# LONGMAN SCHOOL
# ATLAS

AUTHOR  Dr Stephen Scoffham, Canterbury Christ Church University

CHIEF CONSULTANT  Dr David Lambert, Geographical Association

EDITORIAL CONSULTANTS  Paul Baker, Alan Parkinson

The Publisher and author are grateful for additional support and advice from
Dr Chris Young and other colleagues in the Department of Geographical and Life Sciences,
Canterbury Christ Church University.

PEARSON
Longman

# CONTENTS

# INTRODUCTION

An atlas is a book of maps. As well as showing where places are, this atlas considers how places are changing. It invites you to think about some of the key problems and issues facing the world at the moment. The text, charts, diagrams, photographs and satellite images provide extra information to help develop your ideas.

## Using and drawing maps

The maps in this atlas aim to show the world as clearly and accurately as possible. In selecting and presenting information, the map maker has followed a number of rules. Check that you have followed this system when you draw any maps of your own.

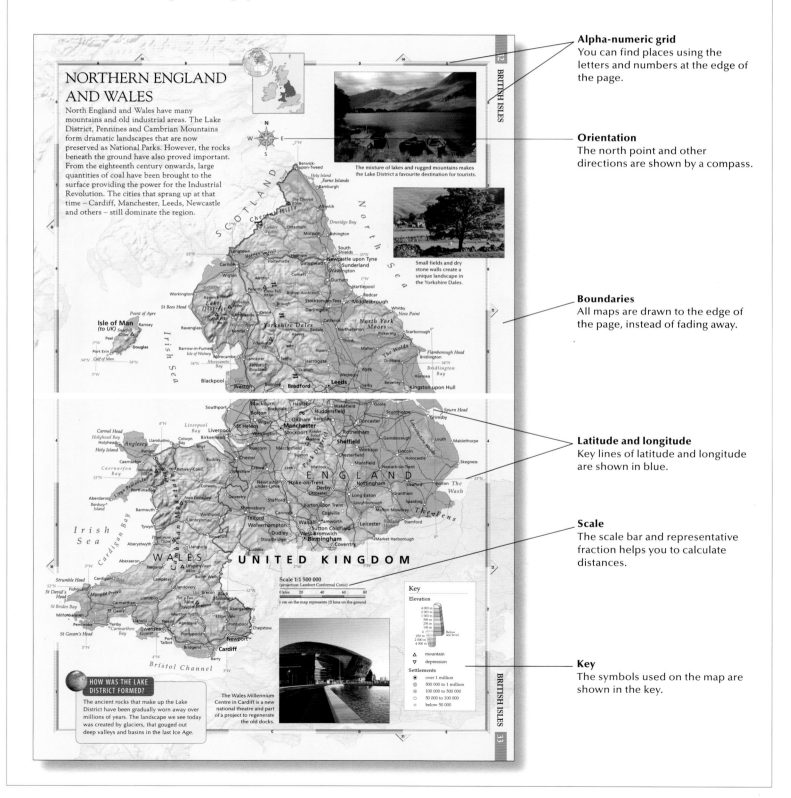

**NORTHERN ENGLAND AND WALES**

North England and Wales have many mountains and old industrial areas. The Lake District, Pennines and Cambrian Mountains form dramatic landscapes that are now preserved as National Parks. However, the rocks beneath the ground have also proved important. From the eighteenth century onwards, large quantities of coal have been brought to the surface providing the power for the Industrial Revolution. The cities that sprang up at that time – Cardiff, Manchester, Leeds, Newcastle and others – still dominate the region.

The mixture of lakes and rugged mountains makes the Lake District a favourite destination for tourists.

Small fields and dry stone walls create a unique landscape in the Yorkshire Dales.

**HOW WAS THE LAKE DISTRICT FORMED?**
The ancient rocks that make up the Lake District have been gradually worn away over millions of years. The landscape we see today was created by glaciers, that gouged out deep valleys and basins in the last Ice Age.

The Wales Millennium Centre in Cardiff is a new national theatre and part of a project to regenerate the old docks.

Scale 1:1 500 000
(projection: Lambert Conformal Conic)
0 kms    20    40    60    80
1 cm on the map represents 15 kms on the ground

**Key**
Elevation
4 000 m
2 000 m
1 000 m
500 m
250 m
100 m
0
250 m
2 000 m
4 000 m
Below sea level
△ mountain
▽ depression
Settlements
⊕ over 1 million
⊙ 500 000 to 1 million
⊙ 100 000 to 500 000
○ 50 000 to 100 000
○ below 50 000

**Alpha-numeric grid**
You can find places using the letters and numbers at the edge of the page.

**Orientation**
The north point and other directions are shown by a compass.

**Boundaries**
All maps are drawn to the edge of the page, instead of fading away.

**Latitude and longitude**
Key lines of latitude and longitude are shown in blue.

**Scale**
The scale bar and representative fraction helps you to calculate distances.

**Key**
The symbols used on the map are shown in the key.

# OUR WORLD

Sometimes it is important to describe exactly where places are on the Earth's surface. Several thousand years ago, the Greeks and Romans developed a system of imaginary grid lines to solve this problem. This was the basis for the modern system of latitude and longitude.

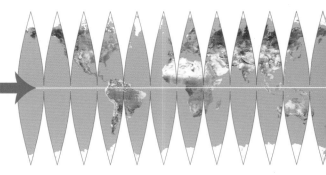

The only really accurate way to show the world is to use a globe. Flat maps always involve distortions but they do have the advantage of showing much more detail. Most of the maps in this atlas use the Eckert IV projection, which distorts area and direction as little as possible.

## Latitude

Lines of latitude circle the Earth, running parallel to each other from east to west. The most famous is the Equator (0 degrees). The latitude of any place on the Earth's surface is the angle between the place you want to describe, the Equator and the centre of the Earth. Latitude is measured in degrees north or south of the Equator.

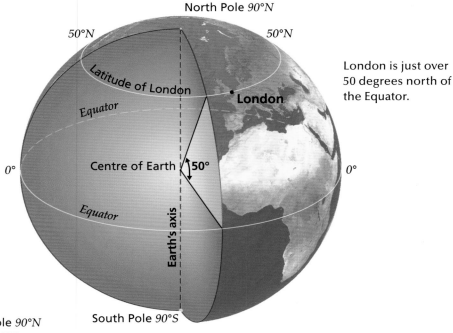

London is just over 50 degrees north of the Equator.

The tilt of the Earth's axis is just over 23 degrees.

## Special lines of latitude

Due to the tilt of the Earth's axis, some lines of latitude have special significance. Between the Tropic of Cancer and Tropic of Capricorn, the sun passes directly overhead at some times of the year. Inside the Arctic and Antarctic Circles, there are 24 hours of sunlight in summer and 24 hours of darkness in winter.

## Longitude

Lines of longitude run from north to south, dividing the world into segments. They are closest together at the Poles and furthest apart at the Equator. The longitude of any place is the angle between the Prime Meridian (0 degrees), the Earth's axis and the place you want to describe. Longitude is measured in degrees east or west of the Prime Meridian which, by convention, passes through Greenwich in London.

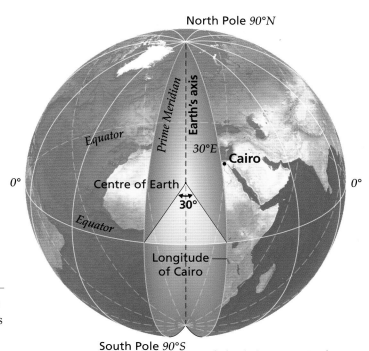

Cairo is just over 30 degrees east of the Prime Meridian.

## Time

Lines of longitude are important because they can be used to measure the spinning of the Earth, the basis for time. Places to the east of the Prime Meridian have an earlier sunrise than those to the west. The time changes exactly one hour for every 15 degrees of longitude. This explains why large countries are divided into time zones and why people who go on long journeys have to adjust their clocks.

## International time zones

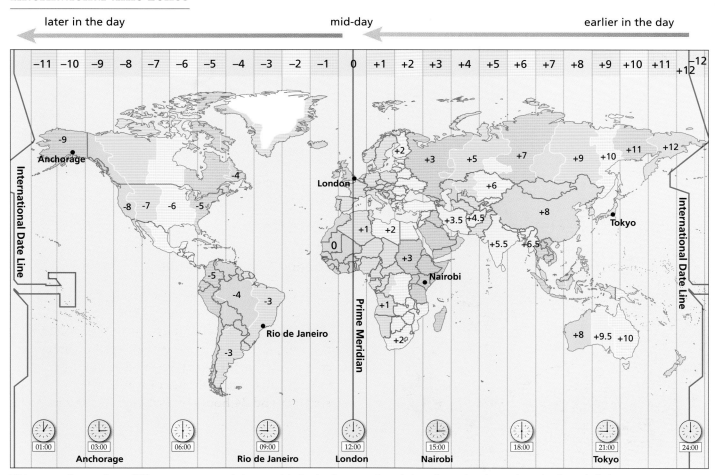

This map shows time differences around the world. At the international date line, the time changes by a full day.

# POLITICAL

This map is called a political map because it shows different countries. At the moment there are almost 200 countries in the world, but the number of countries keeps changing as governments decide on different borders. Some borders follow physical features, such as rivers or mountain ranges. Others are long and straight because they follow lines of latitude or longitude. Borders often mark a change of language or culture.

### What is a country?

All countries have a capital city, their own flag and symbols to represent their identity. However, countries vary greatly in size ranging from small islands, like Sri Lanka, to vast territories, such as Canada and the Russian Federation.

### Scale at Equator 1:89 300 000
(projection: Eckert IV)

| 0 kms | 1 000 | 2 000 | 3 000 | 4 000 | 5 000 |
|---|---|---|---|---|---|

1 cm on the map represents 893 kms on the ground

### Key

Borders

——— international border

- - - - disputed border

——— maritime border

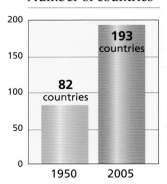

### Number of countries

The break up of colonial empires around the world since 1950 has led to a huge increase in the number of countries.

**DISCUSSION**

Which continent has the most countries?

How many countries do you think there might be in 50 years' time?

## WEST AFRICA

WESTERN SAHARA (occupied by Morocco)
ALGERIA
LIBYA
*Tropic of Cancer*
MAURITANIA
MALI
NIGER
SENEGAL
GAMBIA
GUINEA-BISSAU
GUINEA
BURKINA
BENIN
TOGO
GHANA
NIGERIA
SIERRA LEONE
IVORY COAST
LIBERIA
CAMEROON
EQUATORIAL GUINEA

Scale 1:45 000 000

0 kms   500   1 000   1 500

## EUROPE

NORWAY
SWEDEN
FINLAND
Faeroe Islands
*North Sea*
RUSSIAN FEDERATION
ESTONIA
LATVIA
UNITED KINGDOM
DENMARK
RUSS. FED.
LITHUANIA
IRELAND
NETHERLANDS
POLAND
BELARUS
Channel Islands
BELGIUM
GERMANY
CZECH REPUBLIC
SLOVAKIA
UKRAINE
LUXEMBOURG
SWITZERLAND
AUSTRIA
HUNGARY
MOLDOVA
FRANCE
SLOVENIA
CROATIA
ROMANIA
BOSNIA & HERZEGOVINA
SERBIA & MONTENEGRO
*Caspian Sea*
BULGARIA
MACEDONIA
ITALY
PORTUGAL
SPAIN
ALBANIA
TURKEY
*Mediterranean Sea*
GREECE
Gibraltar
MALTA
CYPRUS

Scale 1:45 000 000

0 kms   500   1 000   1 500

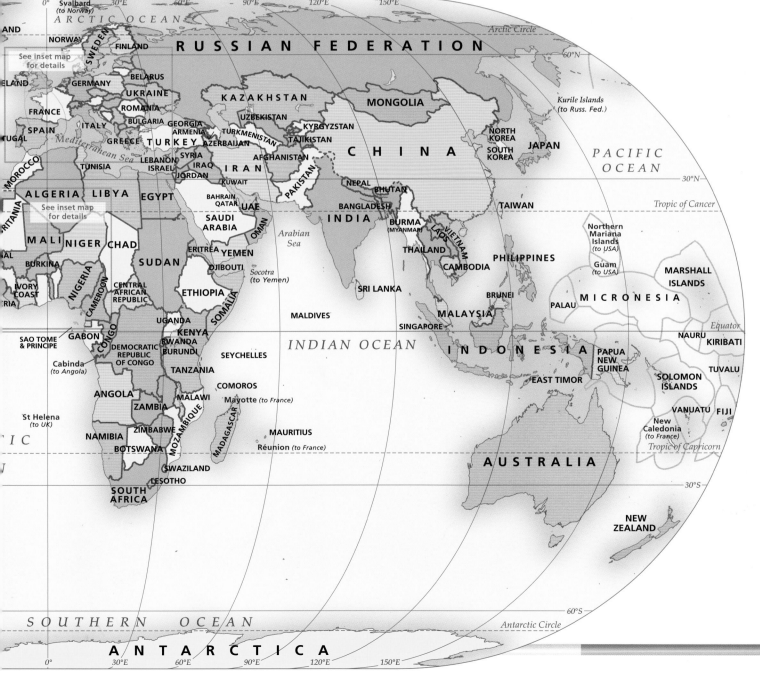

ARCTIC OCEAN
Svalbard (to Norway)
Arctic Circle
NORWAY
SWEDEN
FINLAND
RUSSIAN FEDERATION
See inset map for details
GERMANY
BELARUS
FRANCE
UKRAINE
KAZAKHSTAN
MONGOLIA
Kurile Islands (to Russ. Fed.)
SPAIN
ITALY
ROMANIA
BULGARIA
GEORGIA
ARMENIA
UZBEKISTAN
KYRGYZSTAN
PORTUGAL
*Mediterranean Sea*
GREECE
TURKEY
AZERBAIJAN
TURKMENISTAN
TAJIKISTAN
NORTH KOREA
JAPAN
PACIFIC OCEAN
MOROCCO
TUNISIA
SYRIA
AFGHANISTAN
CHINA
SOUTH KOREA
LEBANON
ISRAEL
IRAQ
IRAN
ALGERIA
LIBYA
EGYPT
JORDAN
KUWAIT
PAKISTAN
NEPAL
BHUTAN
TAIWAN
Tropic of Cancer
See inset map for details
BAHRAIN
QATAR
UAE
BANGLADESH
Northern Mariana Islands (to USA)
MALI
NIGER
CHAD
SAUDI ARABIA
INDIA
BURMA (MYANMAR)
BURKINA
OMAN
*Arabian Sea*
LAOS
VIETNAM
Guam (to USA)
MARSHALL ISLANDS
NIGERIA
SUDAN
ERITREA
YEMEN
THAILAND
CAMBODIA
PHILIPPINES
IVORY COAST
CAMEROON
CENTRAL AFRICAN REPUBLIC
DJIBOUTI
Socotra (to Yemen)
SRI LANKA
BRUNEI
MICRONESIA
SAO TOME & PRINCIPE
GABON
UGANDA
ETHIOPIA
SOMALIA
MALDIVES
MALAYSIA
PALAU
CONGO
DEMOCRATIC REPUBLIC OF CONGO
RWANDA
KENYA
SINGAPORE
INDONESIA
NAURU
KIRIBATI
Cabinda (to Angola)
BURUNDI
SEYCHELLES
INDIAN OCEAN
PAPUA NEW GUINEA
TANZANIA
TUVALU
COMOROS
EAST TIMOR
SOLOMON ISLANDS
ANGOLA
MALAWI
Mayotte (to France)
VANUATU
FIJI
St Helena (to UK)
ZAMBIA
MADAGASCAR
MAURITIUS
New Caledonia (to France)
NAMIBIA
ZIMBABWE
MOZAMBIQUE
Réunion (to France)
Tropic of Capricorn
BOTSWANA
AUSTRALIA
SWAZILAND
LESOTHO
SOUTH AFRICA
30°S
NEW ZEALAND
SOUTHERN OCEAN
Antarctic Circle
ANTARCTICA
60°S

# PHYSICAL

Almost two-thirds of the world's surface is covered by seas and oceans. The other third consists of islands and great blocks of land, known as continents.

## What shapes the Earth's surface?

Some parts of the Earth are being lifted up into jagged mountain ranges. Other areas are being worn away by the action of rivers, ice and the sea. The interaction between mountain building and erosion brings constant changes to the Earth's surface.

### Continent cartogram

EUROPE
13 000 000 sq km

ASIA
44 000 000 sq km

NORTH AMERICA
24 500 000 sq km

AFRICA
30 000 000 sq km

SOUTH AMERICA
18 000 000 sq km

OCEANIA
9 000 000 sq km

ANTARCTICA
14 000 000 sq km

Key

☐ 1 million square kilometres

Instead of showing the shape of the coast, this map shows the area of each continent.

## Key

**Elevation**

4 000 m
2 000 m
1 000 m
500 m
250 m
100 m
0
250 m
2 000 m
4 000 m

Below sea level

△ mountain

▽ depression

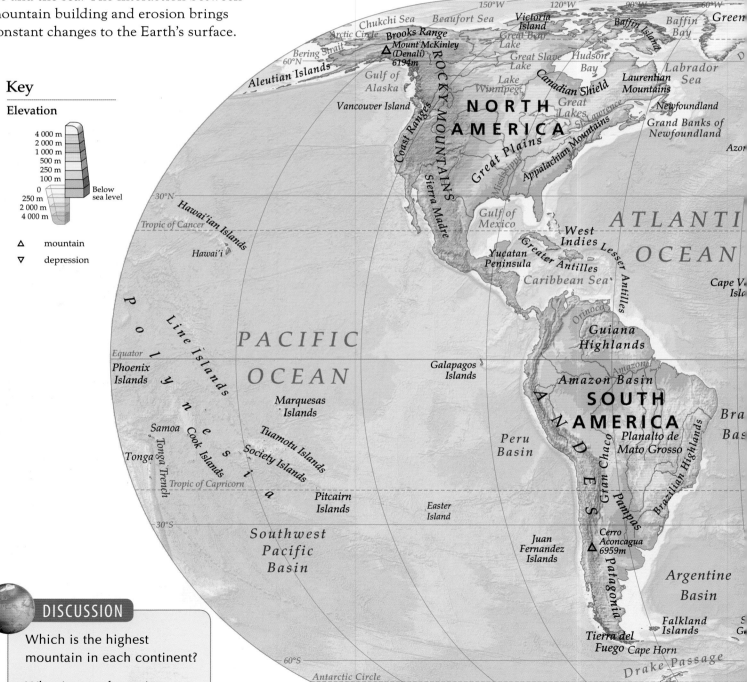

### DISCUSSION

Which is the highest mountain in each continent?

What is your favourite type of scenery?

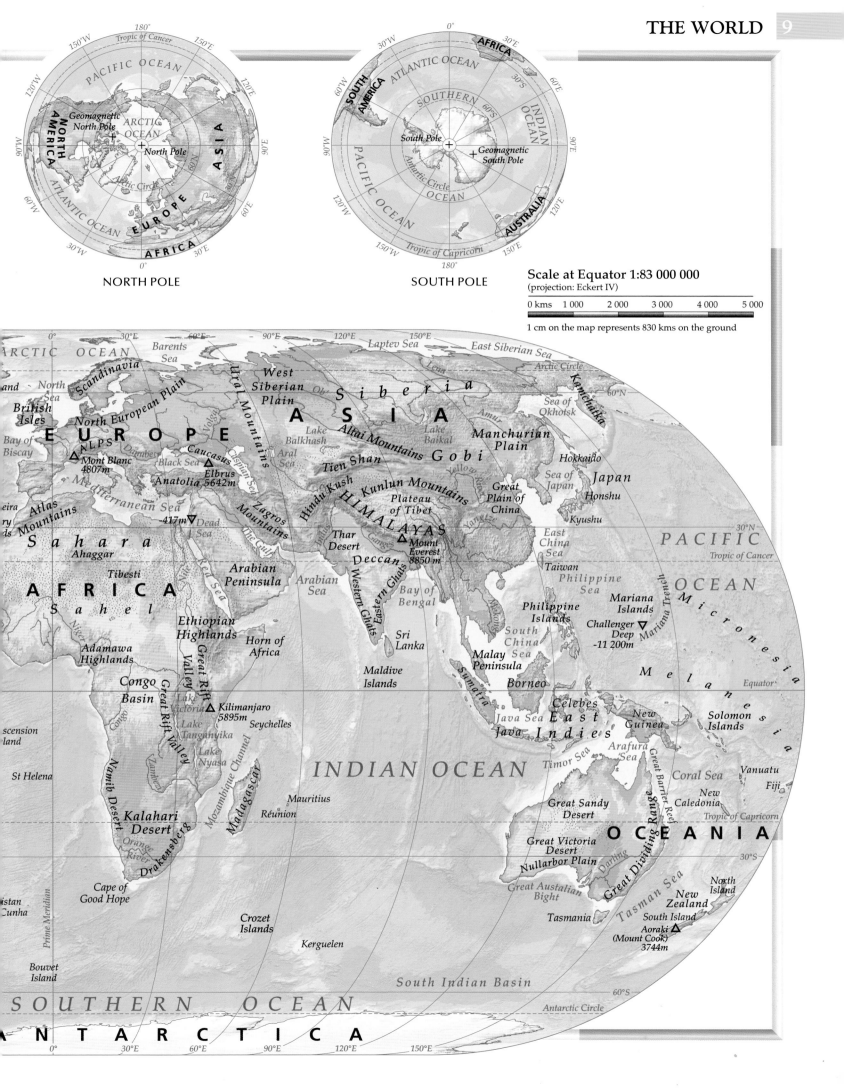

## NORTH POLE

Geomagnetic North Pole
North Pole
PACIFIC OCEAN
Tropic of Cancer
ARCTIC OCEAN
NORTH AMERICA
ASIA
EUROPE
ATLANTIC OCEAN
Arctic Circle
AFRICA

## SOUTH POLE

AFRICA
ATLANTIC OCEAN
SOUTH AMERICA
SOUTHERN OCEAN
South Pole
Geomagnetic South Pole
INDIAN OCEAN
Antarctic Circle
PACIFIC OCEAN
AUSTRALIA
Tropic of Capricorn

### Scale at Equator 1:83 000 000
(projection: Eckert IV)

0 kms   1 000   2 000   3 000   4 000   5 000

1 cm on the map represents 830 kms on the ground

ARCTIC OCEAN
Barents Sea
Laptev Sea
East Siberian Sea
Arctic Circle
Scandinavia
West Siberian Plain
Siberia
Kamchatka
North Sea
Ob
Lena
60°N
British Isles
North European Plain
Ural Mountains
A S I A
Amur
Sea of Okhotsk
EUROPE
Volga
Lake Balkhash
Altai Mountains
Gobi
Manchurian Plain
Hokkaido
Bay of Biscay
ALPS
Danube
Caucasus
Aral Sea
Lake Baikal
Sea of Japan
Japan
Mont Blanc 4807m
Black Sea
Caspian Sea
Tien Shan
Great Plain of China
Honshu
Elbrus 5642m
Anatolia
Zagros Mountains
Hindu Kush
Kunlun Mountains
Plateau of Tibet
Yellow River
Kyushu
Atlas Mountains
Mediterranean Sea
-417m ▽ Dead Sea
HIMALAYAS
Yangtze
East China Sea
30°N
Sahara
The Gulf
Red Sea
Thar Desert
Mount Everest 8850 m
Taiwan
PACIFIC OCEAN
Ahaggar
Arabian Peninsula
Indus
Ganges
Deccan
Philippine Sea
Tropic of Cancer
Tibesti
Arabian Sea
Western Ghats
Eastern Ghats
Bay of Bengal
Philippine Islands
Mariana Islands
Mariana Trench
A F R I C A
Sahel
Ethiopian Highlands
Horn of Africa
Sri Lanka
South China Sea
Challenger Deep -11 200m
Micronesia
Adamawa Highlands
Niger
Great Rift Valley
Maldive Islands
Malay Peninsula
Melanesia
Congo Basin
Great Rift Valley
Lake Victoria
Kilimanjaro 5895m
Seychelles
Sumatra
Borneo
Celebes
New Guinea
Solomon Islands
Equator
scension land
Congo
Lake Tanganyika
Java Sea
East Indies
St Helena
Lake Nyasa
Java
Arafura Sea
Coral Sea
Vanuatu
Namib Desert
Zambezi
Mozambique Channel
Madagascar
INDIAN OCEAN
Timor Sea
Great Barrier Reef
New Caledonia
Fiji
Mauritius
Réunion
Great Sandy Desert
Tropic of Capricorn
Kalahari Desert
O C E A N I A
Cape of Good Hope
Orange River
Drakensberg
Great Victoria Desert
Nullarbor Plain
Great Dividing Range
Darling
New Zealand
North Island
istan Cunha
Crozet Islands
Great Australian Bight
Tasman Sea
Tasmania
New Zealand
Bouvet Island
Kerguelen
South Island
Aoraki (Mount Cook) 3744m
60°S
Prime Meridian
South Indian Basin
Antarctic Circle
S O U T H E R N   O C E A N
A N T A R C T I C A

# CLIMATE

There are great variations in weather across the Earth's surface. Rain and temperature combine in different patterns according to the season. The average weather that affects a place over a number of years is called the climate.

## Why do climates change?

The Sun provides the energy that drives the world's climate. Generally, the hottest places are near the Equator where the Sun is overhead. By contrast, the coldest places are the polar regions where the Sun is always low in the sky. As the wind and ocean currents distribute the Sun's energy, different climates are created.

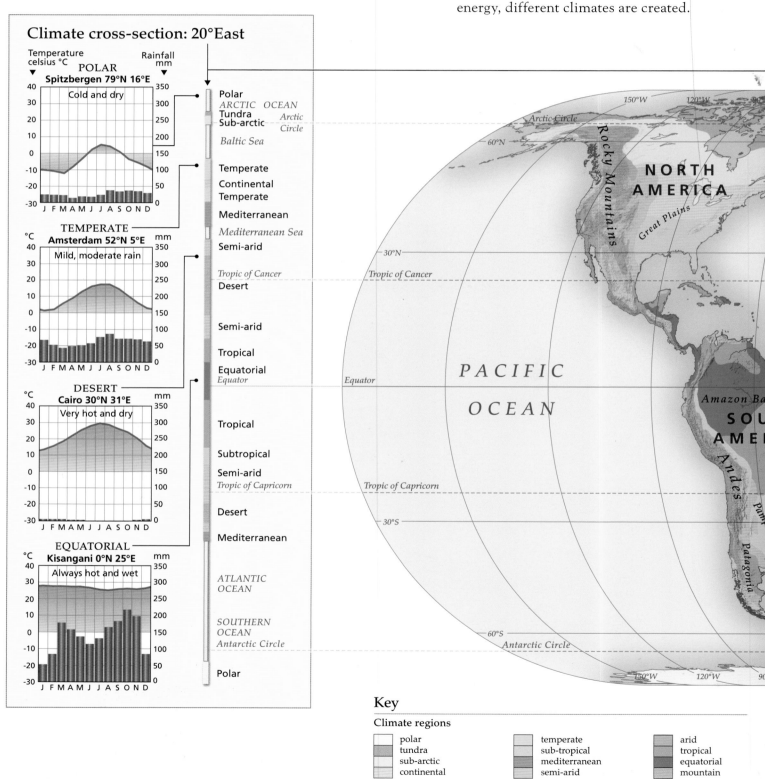

### Climate cross-section: 20°East

**POLAR**
Spitzbergen 79°N 16°E
Cold and dry
Temperature celsius °C / Rainfall mm

**TEMPERATE**
Amsterdam 52°N 5°E
Mild, moderate rain

**DESERT**
Cairo 30°N 31°E
Very hot and dry

**EQUATORIAL**
Kisangani 0°N 25°E
Always hot and wet

Cross-section labels:
Polar
ARCTIC OCEAN
Tundra — Arctic Circle
Sub-arctic
Baltic Sea
Temperate
Continental
Temperate
Mediterranean
Mediterranean Sea
Semi-arid
Tropic of Cancer
Desert
Semi-arid
Tropical
Equatorial
Equator
Tropical
Subtropical
Semi-arid
Tropic of Capricorn
Desert
Mediterranean
ATLANTIC OCEAN
SOUTHERN OCEAN
Antarctic Circle
Polar

Map labels:
NORTH AMERICA
Rocky Mountains
Great Plains
PACIFIC OCEAN
Amazon Ba[sin]
SOUTH AMER[ICA]
Andes
Pam[pas]
Patagonia
Arctic Circle
Tropic of Cancer
Equator
Tropic of Capricorn
Antarctic Circle
150°W, 120°W, 90°W
60°N, 30°N, 30°S, 60°S

## Key

**Climate regions**

| | | |
|---|---|---|
| polar | temperate | arid |
| tundra | sub-tropical | tropical |
| sub-arctic | mediterranean | equatorial |
| continental | semi-arid | mountain |

Ocean currents move heat around the world. This satellite image shows the temperature of surface water in May. Note especially the cold current on the west coast of South America and the relatively warm seas around the UK.

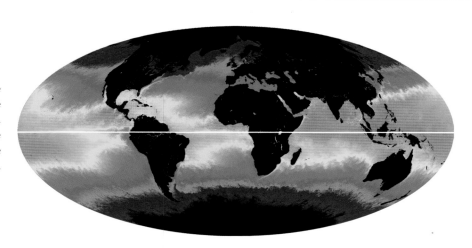

— Climate cross-section: 20°East

**Scale at Equator 1:113 000 000**
(projection: Eckert IV)

0 kms    2 000    4 000    6 000

1 cm on the map represents 1 130 kms on the ground

## DISCUSSION

What places have the same type of climate as the UK?

Which type of climate do you think is best?

# CLIMATE CHANGE

The evidence from plants, ice cores, rocks and soils shows that the Earth's climate is always changing. At different times in the past, the Earth has been both much warmer and much colder than it is today. These changes can happen gradually over thousands of years, or rapidly over a few decades.

## What is global warming?

Scientists are now convinced that the world's climate is getting warmer. They have detected a steady increase in the amount of carbon dioxide and other gases in the atmosphere that trap the heat of the sun. Some nations regard global warming as a very serious threat and have signed the Kyoto Agreement to stabilise and eventually lower air pollution levels.

## Greenhouse gases

**Carbon dioxide levels**
(parts per million)

Carbon dioxide is one of the main causes of global warming. The quantity of carbon dioxide in the atmosphere has increased steadily since the Industrial Revolution in 1850. Levels are expected to go on increasing.

## The impact of global warming

It is impossible to predict exactly how fast temperatures will rise and how global warming will affect us. The map and text boxes show some of the possibilities.

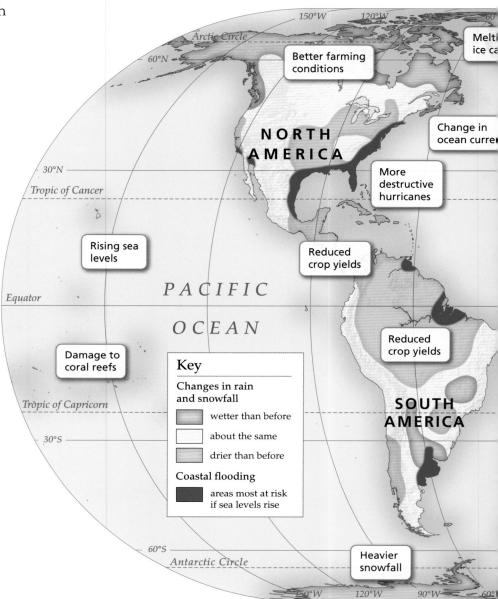

Better farming conditions

Melti ice ca

Change in ocean curre

More destructive hurricanes

Rising sea levels

Reduced crop yields

Reduced crop yields

Damage to coral reefs

**Key**

**Changes in rain and snowfall**

- wetter than before
- about the same
- drier than before

**Coastal flooding**

- areas most at risk if sea levels rise

Heavier snowfall

### Sea levels

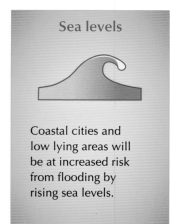

Coastal cities and low lying areas will be at increased risk from flooding by rising sea levels.

### Tropical storms

Intense tropical storms are likely to increase damage to crops and buildings.

### Crop yields

The change in the climate may make farming harder in the Tropics, but could improve growing conditions in higher latitudes.

Global warming "is the most serious threat that humanity has faced in all its recorded history".

Lord May, leading UK scientist

**Scale at Equator 1:113 000 000**
(projection: Eckert IV)

| 0 kms | 2 000 | 4 000 | 6 000 |

1 cm on the map represents 1 130 kms on the ground

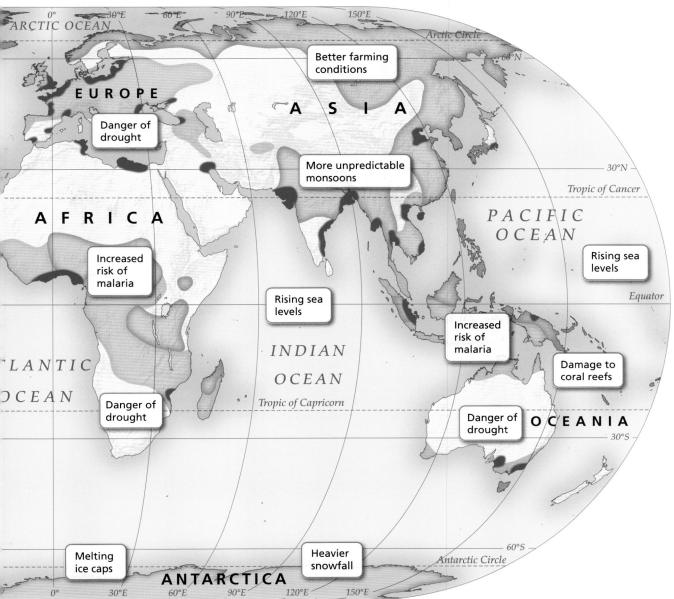

ARCTIC OCEAN

Arctic Circle

EUROPE

ASIA

Better farming conditions

60°N

Danger of drought

More unpredictable monsoons

30°N

Tropic of Cancer

AFRICA

PACIFIC OCEAN

Increased risk of malaria

Rising sea levels

Rising sea levels

Equator

ATLANTIC OCEAN

INDIAN OCEAN

Increased risk of malaria

Damage to coral reefs

Danger of drought

Tropic of Capricorn

Danger of drought

OCEANIA

30°S

Melting ice caps

Heavier snowfall

60°S

Antarctic Circle

ANTARCTICA

0°    30°E    60°E    90°E    120°E    150°E

## Plants and animals

Plants and animals could die out, unable to migrate or adapt to new conditions.

## Fresh water

The shortage of fresh water in some areas may lead to new wars and conflicts.

## Pests and diseases

Malaria and other tropical diseases are expected to spread to new areas as temperatures rise.

### DISCUSSION

How much have carbon dioxide levels increased since 1700?

Which countries and areas do you think might suffer most from global warming? Which areas might benefit?

# NATURAL DISASTERS

Violent or unexpected changes often happen to the Earth's surface. When they kill people they are known as natural disasters. Natural disasters include droughts, floods, storms, earthquakes and volcanic eruptions. As the world population grows larger, deaths and damage from natural disasters are increasing. However, better communications are making us more aware of the risks.

## Volcanoes

The molten rock deep within the Earth breaks out onto the surface in volcanoes. Many volcanoes are harmless, but when they erupt the force can devastate large areas and poisonous gas spreads high into the sky.

## Earthquakes

Earthquakes happen when the different parts of the Earth's crust collide, slide into each other or tear apart. When the epicentre is near a town or city many people can be killed. If the earthquake sets off a tsunami, or tidal wave, it can cause even more damage.

This sequence of photographs shows what happened in less than a minute when Mt St Helens erupted on May 18th, 1980.

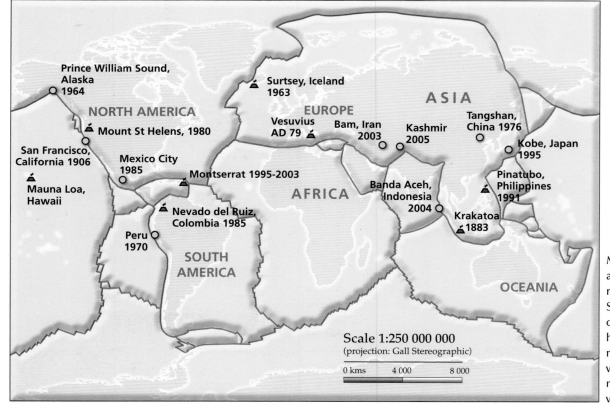

Prince William Sound, Alaska
○ 1964

NORTH AMERICA

Mount St Helens, 1980

San Francisco, California 1906

Mexico City 1985

Mauna Loa, Hawaii

Montserrat 1995-2003

Nevado del Ruiz, Colombia 1985

Peru ○ 1970

SOUTH AMERICA

Surtsey, Iceland 1963

EUROPE

Vesuvius AD 79

Bam, Iran 2003

Kashmir 2005

ASIA

Tangshan, China 1976

Kobe, Japan 1995

AFRICA

Banda Aceh, Indonesia 2004

Pinatubo, Philippines 1991

Krakatoa 1883

OCEANIA

### Key

⛰ major volcanic event
○ major earthquake
— plate boundary

Scale 1:250 000 000
(projection: Gall Stereographic)

0 kms    4 000    8 000

Most earthquakes and volcanoes occur near plate boundaries. Some volcanoes erupt continually and there are hundreds of minor earth movements around the world every day. This map shows some of the well-known events.

## Droughts

Long periods with very little rain are known as droughts. Trees and plants shrivel without water and people and animals struggle to get enough to drink. Sometimes the desert spreads over the parched land, increasing the damage.

## Tropical storms

In the Tropics, the warmth of the sea causes severe storms to develop at certain times of the year. Devastating winds and torrential rain can destroy whole communities and people are killed as buildings collapse.

## Floods

Heavy rain, tidal waves and earthquakes all cause floods. If people are given enough warning they may be able to escape, but houses and crops will still be ruined.

## Tropical storm tracks

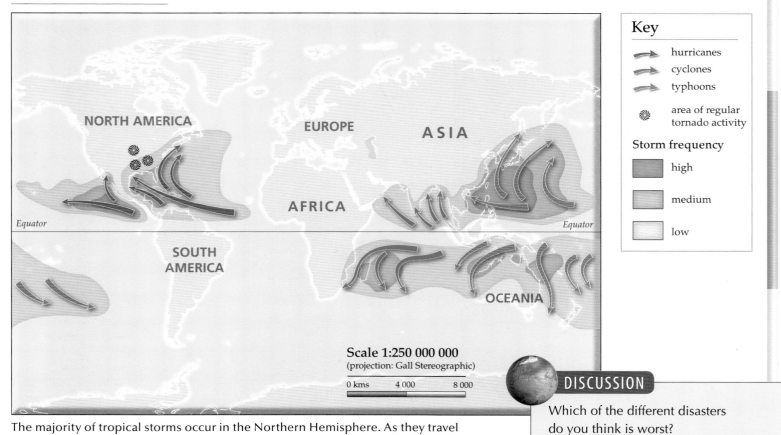

NORTH AMERICA

EUROPE

ASIA

AFRICA

SOUTH AMERICA

OCEANIA

Equator

Equator

### Key

→ hurricanes
→ cyclones
→ typhoons
area of regular tornado activity

**Storm frequency**

high

medium

low

Scale 1:250 000 000
(projection: Gall Stereographic)

0 kms        4 000        8 000

The majority of tropical storms occur in the Northern Hemisphere. As they travel away from the Equator, their direction is deflected by the spinning of the Earth. When the storm reaches land or cooler water, it loses energy and breaks up.

## DISCUSSION

Which of the different disasters do you think is worst?

Why do similar natural disasters result in very different amounts of damage?

# LIFE ON EARTH

Different areas of the Earth have a unique combination of climate, plants and scenery. These are known as biomes. Some biomes, such as tropical rainforests, have a huge variety of plants and creatures. Other biomes such as grasslands and deciduous forests have been greatly altered by human activity.

As well as being enchantingly beautiful, coral reefs provide a habitat for a great number of different plants and creatures.

**Hot desert**

Sahara Desert, Libya, North Africa

**Polar**

Pack ice and icebergs, Arctic Ocean

**Tundra**

Eastern Siberia, Russian Federation

## Key

**World biomes**

- polar
- tundra
- coniferous forest
- deciduous forest
- grassland
- mediterranean
- savanna
- tropical forest
- hot desert
- cold desert
- mountain

Arctic Circle

60°N

NORTH AMERICA

ATLANTIC OCEAN

30°N

Tropic of Cancer

Equator

PACIFIC OCEAN

SOUTH AMERICA

Tropic of Capricorn

30°S

60°S
Antarctic Circle

150°W    120°W    90°W    60°W

**Scale at Equator 1:150 000 000**
(projection: Eckert IV)

0 kms    2 000    4 000    6 000

1 cm on the map represents 1 500 kms on the ground

Around the world, coral reefs are dying as a result of pollution, development, tourism, climate change and the damage caused by fishing.

## Flagship species

Scientists believe that half of all plant and animal species could become extinct in the next 50 years. Conservation groups are focusing their campaigns on a few flagship species which, as well as being at risk themselves, provide an 'umbrella' for other forms of wildlife.

**Flagship species include:**

Giant pandas

Tigers

Whales/dolphins

Rhinos

Elephants

Turtles

Great apes

AT RISK

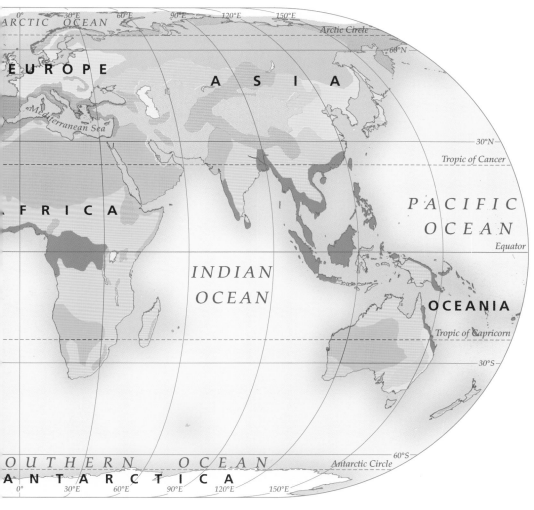

Deciduous forest

Burnham Beeches,
Buckinghamshire, UK

Tropical rainforest

Rancho Grande, Venezuela,
South America

Savanna

Tarangire National Park,
Tanzania, East Africa

## DISCUSSION

Which other parts of the world have the same biome as the UK?

Can human activity ever improve a biome?

# THREATENED ENVIRONMENTS

The environment has suffered as people use the Earth's resources for industry, farming and leisure. Pollution and the loss of plant and animal life are now widespread.

## Disappearing forests

Around the world forests are shrinking as timber is cut down and land is cleared for farming. In Europe, the temperate forests were cut down centuries ago. The rainforests, which are home to a great number of different plants and creatures, are now particularly at risk.

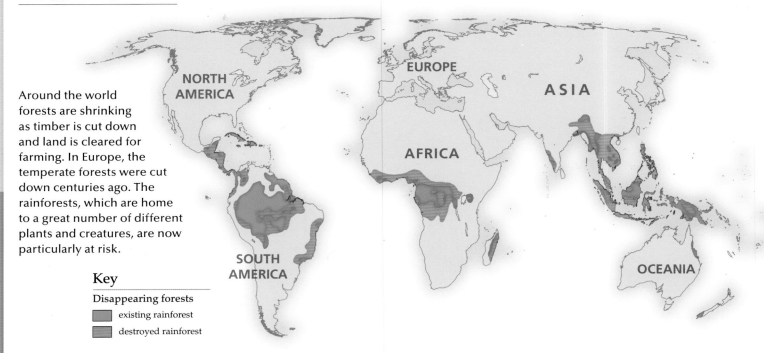

**Key**

Disappearing forests

existing rainforest

destroyed rainforest

## Desertification

Around the world dry areas are becoming deserts as people put more and more pressure on the land. Climate change, overgrazing and clearing wood for firewood are all making the problem worse.

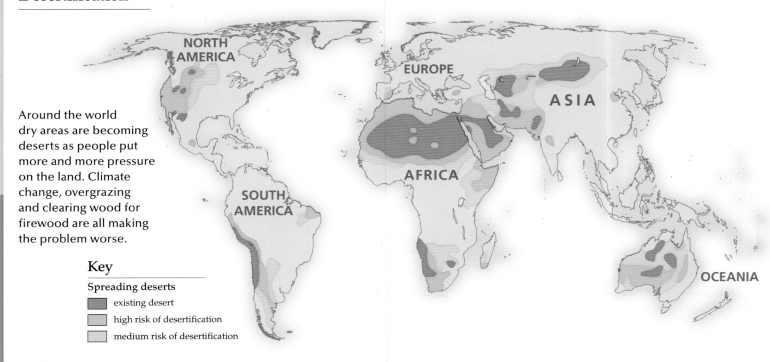

**Key**

Spreading deserts

existing desert

high risk of desertification

medium risk of desertification

# Water pollution

Pollution affects many rivers, seas and oceans. Some coastlines are being damaged by waste from factories, farms and cities. Oil pollution is another problem, especially in busy shipping lanes.

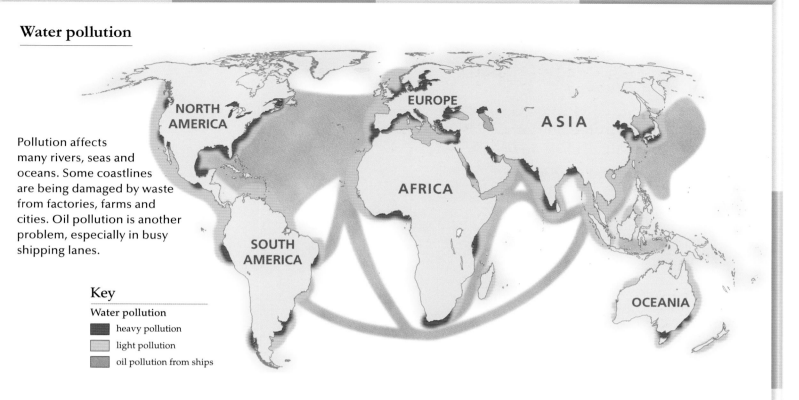

### Key

**Water pollution**

- heavy pollution
- light pollution
- oil pollution from ships

# Air pollution

Acid rain is caused by the sulphur and nitrogen that is released from burning coal, oil and gas. The acid can kill trees and plants as well as fish in rivers and lakes.

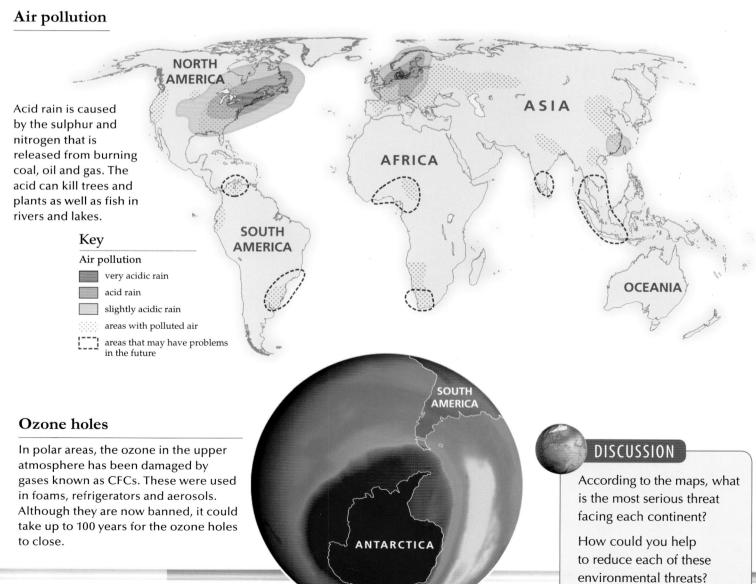

### Key

**Air pollution**

- very acidic rain
- acid rain
- slightly acidic rain
- areas with polluted air
- areas that may have problems in the future

# Ozone holes

In polar areas, the ozone in the upper atmosphere has been damaged by gases known as CFCs. These were used in foams, refrigerators and aerosols. Although they are now banned, it could take up to 100 years for the ozone holes to close.

## DISCUSSION

According to the maps, what is the most serious threat facing each continent?

How could you help to reduce each of these environmental threats?

# POPULATION

The number of people in the world has trebled in the last 100 years. Numbers are expected to go on rising throughout this century. However, the rate of increase will slow down and some regions, such as southeast Europe, may actually become emptier.

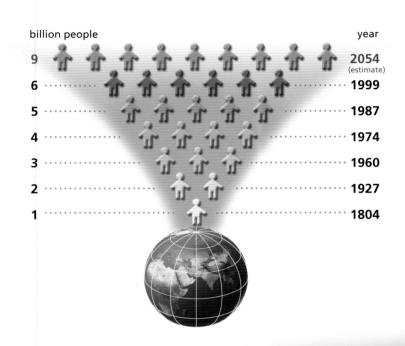

| billion people | | year |
|---|---|---|
| 9 | | **2054** (estimate) |
| 6 | | **1999** |
| 5 | | **1987** |
| 4 | | **1974** |
| 3 | | **1960** |
| 2 | | **1927** |
| 1 | | **1804** |

## World's most populous countries: 2005

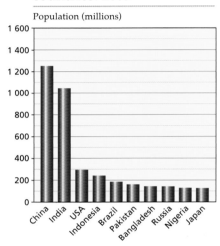

Population (millions)

At present, seven out of ten of the world's most populous countries are in Asia.

## World's most populous countries: 2050

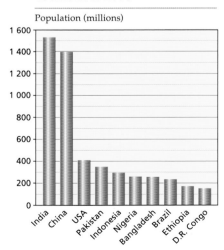

Population (millions)

By 2050 the population of countries in south Asia and parts of central Africa will have grown considerably.

## Key

### Population density
(people per square km)

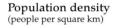

- more than 200
- 100 to 200
- 50 to 100
- 10 to 50
- 1 to 10
- less than 1

● cities with over 10 million people (population in millions)

Source: Th. Brinkhoff: The Principal Agglomerations of the World, http://www.citypopulation.de, 2005-10-01

New York **22m**

Los Angeles **18m**

Mexico City **23m**

Rio de Janeiro **12m**

São Paulo **20m**

Buenos Aires **13m**

## Why do populations change?

The main three factors that affect the population of a country are:

- Life expectancy. Better diet and healthcare mean that people are living longer than in the past.

- Family size. As living conditions improve, many people are choosing to have smaller families.

- Migration. Some people decide to move abroad while others arrive from foreign countries.

## Population cartogram

This cartogram shows countries according to their population. It is possible to compare the number of people without thinking about the size of the country.

## Key

Country area proportional to population

▪ 1 million people

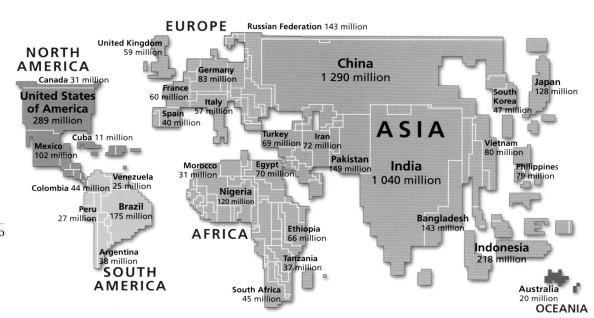

NORTH AMERICA

EUROPE
Russian Federation 143 million
United Kingdom 59 million
Canada 31 million
Germany 83 million
France 60 million
Italy 57 million
Spain 40 million

United States of America 289 million

Mexico 102 million

Cuba 11 million

Colombia 44 million
Venezuela 25 million
Peru 27 million
Brazil 175 million

Argentina 38 million
SOUTH AMERICA

Morocco 31 million
Nigeria 120 million
AFRICA
Egypt 70 million
Ethiopia 66 million
Tanzania 37 million
South Africa 45 million

China 1 290 million
ASIA
Turkey 69 million
Iran 72 million
Pakistan 149 million
India 1 040 million
Bangladesh 143 million

South Korea 47 million
Japan 128 million
Vietnam 80 million
Philippines 79 million

Indonesia 218 million

Australia 20 million
OCEANIA

London 12m
Moscow 14m
Istanbul 11m
Tehran 12m
Cairo 15m
Karachi 14m
Dhaka 13m
Mumbai 20m
Delhi 20m
Kolkata 15m
Beijing 12m
Seoul 22m
Tokyo 35m
Osaka 17m
Shanghai 18m
Shenzhen 10m
Manila 15m
Lagos 11m
Jakarta 17m

**Scale at Equator 1:99 700 000**
(projection: Eckert IV)

| 0 kms | 1 500 | 3 000 | 4 500 | 6 000 |

1 cm on the map represents 997 kms on the ground

### DISCUSSION

Which two continents have the smallest populations (apart from Antarctica)?

How might an increase or decrease in population affect a country?

# GLOBALISATION

The world is linked together by patterns of trade and communication. These links mean that many of the things that we use or see in the shops are imported from other countries. Over the past few decades, there has been a huge increase in the exchange of goods, services and technology around the world. This process is known as globalisation.

## World breakfast

People have been exchanging food and goods for thousands of years. However, since the sixteenth century and Christopher Columbus' voyage across the Atlantic sugar, cotton, coffee, tea and other crops have been grown on plantations. Today, nearly all farmers are locked into a system of world agriculture.

## Trade power

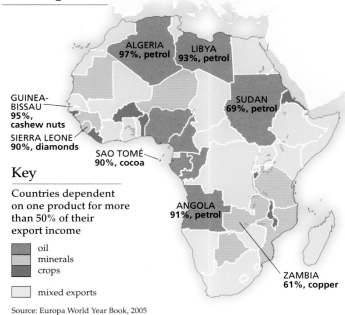

GUINEA-BISSAU
95%, cashew nuts

SIERRA LEONE
90%, diamonds

ALGERIA
97%, petrol

LIBYA
93%, petrol

SUDAN
69%, petrol

SAO TOMÉ
90%, cocoa

ANGOLA
91%, petrol

ZAMBIA
61%, copper

### Key

Countries dependent on one product for more than 50% of their export income

- oil
- minerals
- crops

- mixed exports

Source: Europa World Year Book, 2005

Many African countries earn more than half their export income from just one product, such as petrol or metal ore. This makes them very vulnerable to price changes and unexpected events.

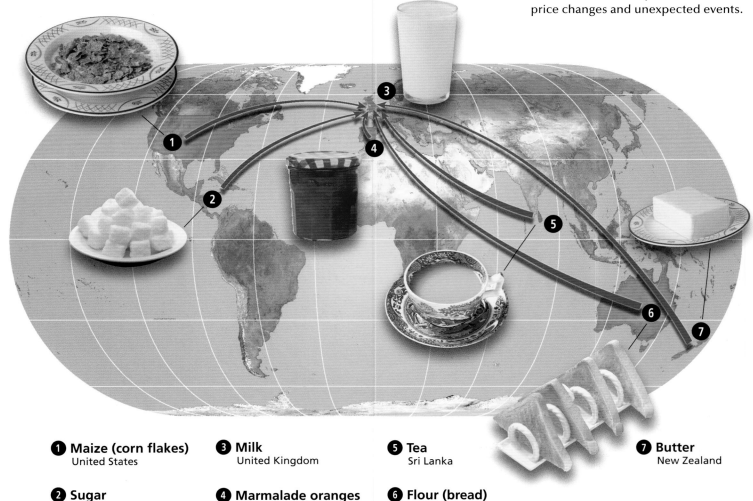

**1** **Maize (corn flakes)**
United States

**2** **Sugar**
Jamaica

**3** **Milk**
United Kingdom

**4** **Marmalade oranges**
Spain

**5** **Tea**
Sri Lanka

**6** **Flour (bread)**
Australia

**7** **Butter**
New Zealand

## Why has globalisation happened?

Globalisation allows companies to take advantage of resources, skills and cheaper labour costs in LEDCs. It also means people can eat fruit and vegetables even when they are out of season. The expansion of air travel and the development of the Internet have made global communications easier than ever before. This too has helped to bind countries together.

## World computer

Computers are made from lots of different parts. The map below provides information about an American company. The computers that it sells are made from parts that come from all over the world. Altogether about 400 companies are involved in supplying components. Many of these are in Asia.

Transnational companies (TNCs) are huge businesses that operate in many countries around the world. Some TNCs help to develop the country's economy, whilst others can exploit low-paid workers.

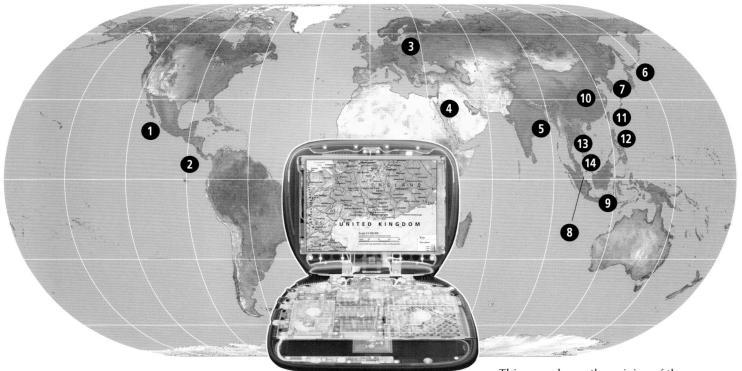

**1 Mexico:**
Battery

**2 Costa Rica:**
Microprocessor

**3 Germany:**
Memory

**4 Israel:**
Memory stick

**5 India:**
Power cord

**6 Japan:**
Memory
LCD display

**7 Korea:**
Memory
LCD display

**8 Singapore:**
Hard disc

**9 Indonesia:**
CD/DVD drive

**10 China:**
Keyboard
Microprocessor
Graphics card
Motherboard
Wireless card
Modem
Battery
CD/DVD drive
Power cord
Power adaptor

**11 Taiwan:**
Memory
Cooling fan
Motherboard
LCD display
Wireless card
Hard disc

**12 Philippines:**
Microprocessor
CD/DVD drive

**13 Thailand:**
Hard disc
Power adaptor

**14 Malaysia:**
Micoprocessor
Wireless card
CD/DVD drive
Memory stick
Battery
Power cord

This map shows the origins of the main components for computers assembled in Malaysia.

### DISCUSSION

What evidence for globalisation can you see in your classroom?

What do you think are the advantages and disadvantages of globalisation?

# UK POLITICAL

This map shows how the United Kingdom is split into four nations and the administrative regions. The counties that are found in many rural areas date back hundreds of years.

**SHETLAND ISLANDS**

Shetland Islands

Scale as main map

**Scale 1:3 750 000**

0 kms    50    100    150

Orkney Islands

3°W

4°W

6°W

Western Isles

58°N

58°N

Moray

Aberdeenshire

2°W

Highland

S C O T L A N D

Angus

Perth and Kinross

Fife

Argyll and Bute

Stirling

East Lothian

56°N

56°N

1°W

2°W

60°N

60°N

1°W

North Ayrshire

South Lanarkshire

Scottish Borders

8°W

East Ayrshire

South Ayrshire

Dumfries and Galloway

Northumberland

NORTHERN IRELAND

North Sea

Strabane

Omagh

Dungannon

Fermanagh

Armagh

Durham

U N I T E D

Cumbria

0°

K I N G D O M

North Yorkshire

East Riding of Yorkshire

54°N

54°N

Newry and Mourne

Isle of Man (to UK)

Lancashire

8°W

6°W

North Lincolnshire

## Key

### Borders

——— international border

——— national border

——— county or unitary authority border

### Countries

England

Scotland

Wales

Northern Ireland

There are over 200 administrative regions in the United Kingdom. Only some of them can be shown on the map.

**DISCUSSION**

Why are some administrative regions so much larger than others?

Isle of Anglesey

Gwynedd

Conwy

Cheshire

Derbyshire

Nottinghamshire

Lincolnshire

2°E

Irish Sea

Powys

Shropshire

Staffordshire

Leicestershire

Norfolk

Ceredigion

WALES

E N G L A N D

Warwickshire

Northamptonshire

Cambridgeshire

Suffolk

52°N

Carmarthenshire

Worcestershire

Herefordshire

Oxfordshire

Bedfordshire

Hertfordshire

Essex

Pembrokeshire

Gloucestershire

Buckinghamshire

Greater London

West Berkshire

Wiltshire

Hampshire

Surrey

Kent

Somerset

West Sussex

East Sussex

Devon

Dorset

Isle of Wight

0°

6°W

English Channel

Cornwall

Isles of Scilly

50°N

50°N

6°W

4°W

2°W

# UK PHYSICAL

The British Isles consists of over 900 islands. Many of them are small but the biggest, Britain, is the eighth largest island in the world. Although surrounded by water, the British Isles has similar rocks to neighbouring countries in Europe. Indeed, Britain only became separated from France about 8500 years ago when the sea flooded the Strait of Dover.

## Scale 1:3 750 000

0 kms     50     100     150

## Key

### Elevation

4 000 m
2 000 m
1 000 m
500 m
250 m
100 m
0
250 m
2 000 m        Below
4 000 m        sea level

△  mountain
▽  depression

## Definitions

**United Kingdom:** England, Scotland, Wales and Northern Ireland

**British Isles:** A group of islands off the northwest coast of Europe

**Great Britain or Britain:** England, Wales and Scotland

## BRITISH ISLES FACTS

**HIGHEST MOUNTAIN:** Ben Nevis  1 343 m

**LONGEST RIVER:** River Severn  322 km

**BIGGEST LAKE:** Lough Neagh  396 sq km

**BIGGEST ISLANDS:** Britain  218 595 sq km, Ireland  84 079 sq km

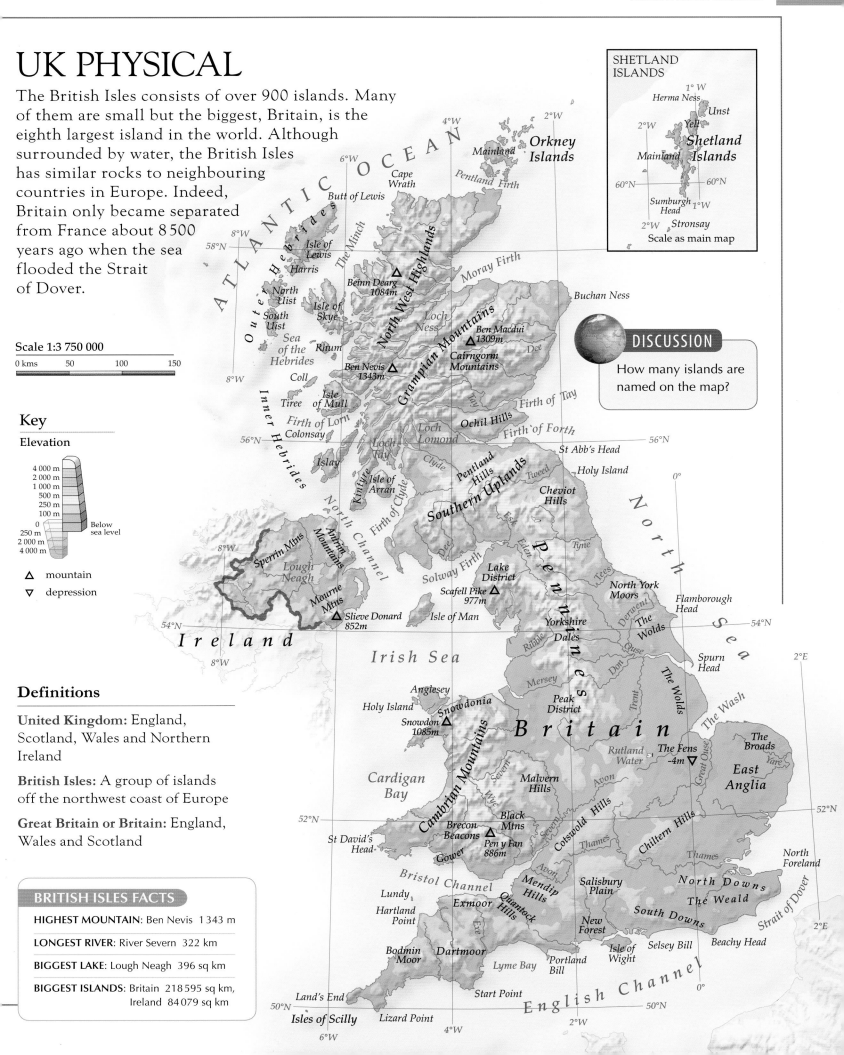

DISCUSSION

How many islands are named on the map?

# UK POPULATION

The population of the UK is unevenly distributed. One third of the UK's population live in southeast England where there are more opportunities for work. London is the largest city in the UK with a population of nearly 12 million people. The emptiest areas are in Scotland where the mountains, moors and remote islands pose problems for housing development.

## Issues for the future

- The population of the UK is expected to reach a maximum of 67 million in 2050.

- Over the last century, more people have left Britain to live abroad than have arrived from overseas.

- 33 New Towns have been created since 1946.

- Around London, major new developments are planned at Ashford, Stevenage, the M11 corridor and Thames Gateway.

## Key

**Population density**
(people per square km)

- above 200
- 100 to 200
- 50 to 100
- 10 to 50
- 1 to 10

**Major settlements**

- ■ ⊙ above 1 million
- ◎ 500 000 to 1 million
- ⊙ below 500 000

A red square indicates a national capital

**Scale 1:5 000 000**

0 kms   50   100   150

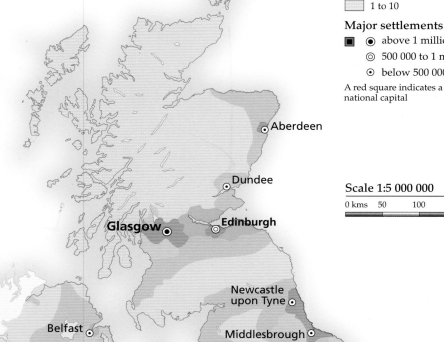

## Population growth

200 years ago most people lived in villages. Today many of these villages have grown larger or changed into towns. Instead of farming the land, people now provide services or process information.

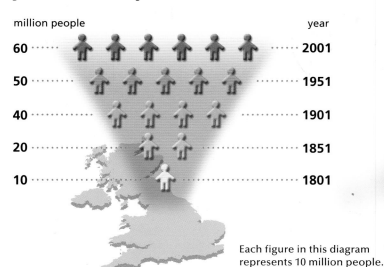

| million people | | year |
|---|---|---|
| 60 | | 2001 |
| 50 | | 1951 |
| 40 | | 1901 |
| 20 | | 1851 |
| 10 | | 1801 |

Each figure in this diagram represents 10 million people.

## DISCUSSION

Why do people move from one part of the world to another?

# UK TRANSPORT

In the UK most people travel by car. There are over 3 000 km of motorway and 342 000 km of paved road and many country lanes. High speed trains and aircraft also link major cities. Planes and ferries, along with the Channel Tunnel railway, provide links to other parts of Europe.

London is the first city in the UK to introduce a congestion charge to reduce traffic and pollution.

### Issues for the future

- The number of people travelling by train is expected to increase by nearly 20% over the next decade.

- As the demand for flights increases, some airlines plan to use cleaner and quieter aircraft.

- Some cities are setting up tram networks to encourage drivers to use public transport.

This diagram shows the number of kilometres each vehicle will travel if all the passengers pay for a litre of fuel.

**Plane: 80 people**

**Car: 1 person**

**Coach: 25 people**

**Intercity train: 250 people**

Which vehicle creates most pollution?

Scale 1:5 000 000

0 kms    50    100    150

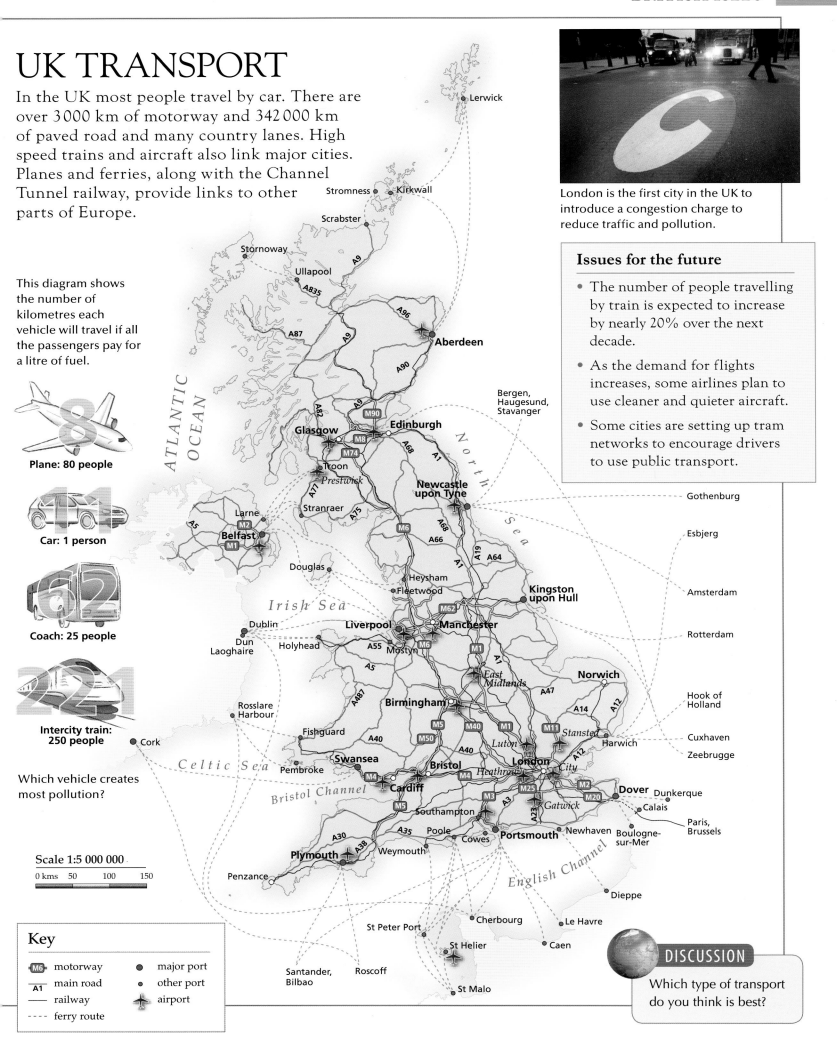

### Key

| | |
|---|---|
| **M6** motorway | ● major port |
| **A1** main road | ∙ other port |
| —— railway | ✈ airport |
| ---- ferry route | |

DISCUSSION

Which type of transport do you think is best?

# UK CLIMATE

The UK has a temperate climate. There are four seasons of roughly equal length, and rain falls throughout the year. Temperatures are moderated by the sea. Find out about the climate in your area from these maps and see how it compares to other parts of the UK.

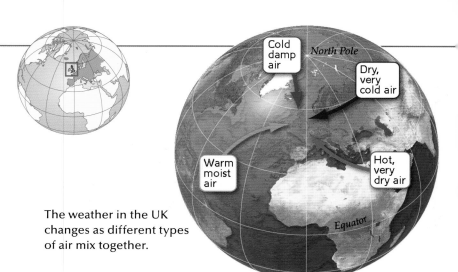

The weather in the UK changes as different types of air mix together.

Cold damp air

Dry, very cold air

North Pole

Warm moist air

Hot, very dry air

Equator

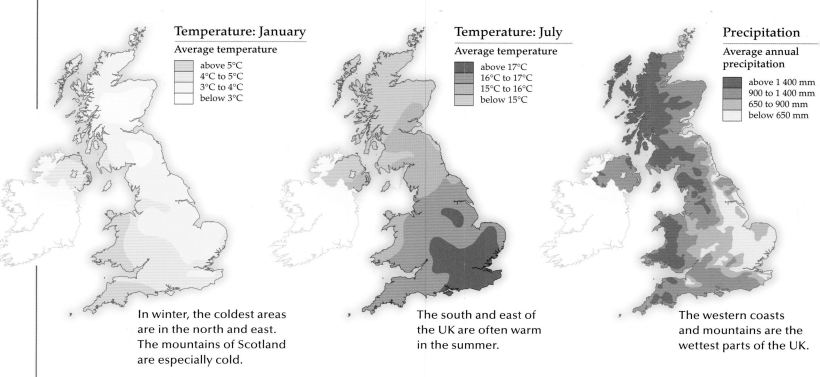

### Temperature: January

**Average temperature**

- above 5°C
- 4°C to 5°C
- 3°C to 4°C
- below 3°C

In winter, the coldest areas are in the north and east. The mountains of Scotland are especially cold.

### Temperature: July

**Average temperature**

- above 17°C
- 16°C to 17°C
- 15°C to 16°C
- below 15°C

The south and east of the UK are often warm in the summer.

### Precipitation

**Average annual precipitation**

- above 1 400 mm
- 900 to 1 400 mm
- 650 to 900 mm
- below 650 mm

The western coasts and mountains are the wettest parts of the UK.

## Unpredictable weather

There have been many extreme weather events in the UK in recent years. Scientists think this may be the result of global warming.

**2005** Severe storms bring flash floods to Carlisle

### Issues for the future

- There are more likely to be water shortages as people, farms and factories increase consumption.

- Long periods of hot, sunny weather are leading to dangerous levels of ozone pollution, especially in towns.

- Warmer winters threaten the Scottish skiing industry.

 **DISCUSSION**

Do you think climate changes are affecting the UK for better or worse?

# UK LAND USE

Large areas of the UK are used for farmland. In the southeast, the flatter land and warmer climate favours crops. In the northwest where the climate is damp and cool, grass grows well so farmers raise cattle and sheep. Increasingly large areas are also given over to houses, factories and other types of development.

## Key

**Land use type**

- forest
- pasture
- cropland
- livestock rearing
- hill farming
- market gardening, pigs and poultry
- urban area

**Industry**

- industrial area
- manufacturing centre

## Green belts

Since the Second World War 'green belts' have been set up around many large towns to shield the countryside from development.

### Key

**Green belts**

- urban area
- green belt

Scale 1:5 000 000

0 kms   50   100   150

## Issues for the future

- The Forestry Commission is planting a mixture of trees in new woods to ensure a variety of species.

- The European Union pays farmers to 'set aside' some fields to limit the quantity of food that is grown.

- There are plans to restore derelict land around cities to create new leisure areas.

### DISCUSSION

What do you think are the advantages and disadvantages of 'green belts'?

# SOUTHERN ENGLAND

Southern England is the flattest, richest and most crowded part of the British Isles. Much of the region is drained by the River Thames which rises in the Cotswold Hills and flows through Oxford to London. In the past, boats brought goods up the river, making London the centre of a trading empire. Today, London is a global financial centre and home to people from all over the world.

Every year around 50 000 new homes are built in southern England, putting great pressure on the countryside.

## Key

### Elevation

4 000 m
2 000 m
1 000 m
500 m
250 m
100 m
0
250 m
2 000 m
4 000 m
Below sea level

△ mountain

### Settlements

■ ⊙ over 1 million
◎ 500 000 to 1 million
⊙ 100 000 to 500 000
○ 50 000 to 100 000
○ below 50 000

A red square indicates a national capital

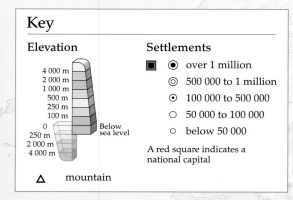

UNITE

Kiddermin

Leominster

Great Malver
Mal
Hi

Hereford

52°N

Ross-on-

Glouce

WALES

Forest of Dean

3°W

Chepstow

3°W

Bristol ⊙

Weston-super-Mare

Bat

Mendip Hills

From

Glastonbury

Bristol Channel

Lundy

Barnstaple Bay

Ilfracombe

Minehead

Dunkery Beacon 519m △

Exmoor

Bridgwater

Hartland Point

Bideford

Barnstaple

Wincanton

51°N

Hartland

Taunton

Yeovil

Torridge

Taw

Exe

Tiverton

Axe

Frome

5°W

Bude Bay

Bridport

Dorch

Boscastle

Okehampton

Exeter

Sidmouth

ATLANTIC

Port Isaac Bay

Tamar

Launceston

High Willhays 621m △

Dartmoor

Weymouth

Dart

Exmouth

Lyme Bay

OCEAN

Padstow

Bodmin Moor

Newton Abbot

Torquay

Portland Bill

Bodmin

Tor Bay

3°W

Newquay

Ligger Bay

Plymouth ⊙

St Austell

Redruth

Truro

St Austell Bay

Dartmouth

St Ives

Salcombe

Start Point

Penzance

Land's End

Falmouth

+ Eddystone Rocks

Helston

Mount's Bay

4°W

50°N

Isles of Scilly

Hugh Town

6°W

5°W

Lizard Point

50°N

## Scale 1:1 500 000
(projection: Lambert Conformal Conic)

0 kms    20    40    60    80

1 cm on the map represents 15 kms on the ground

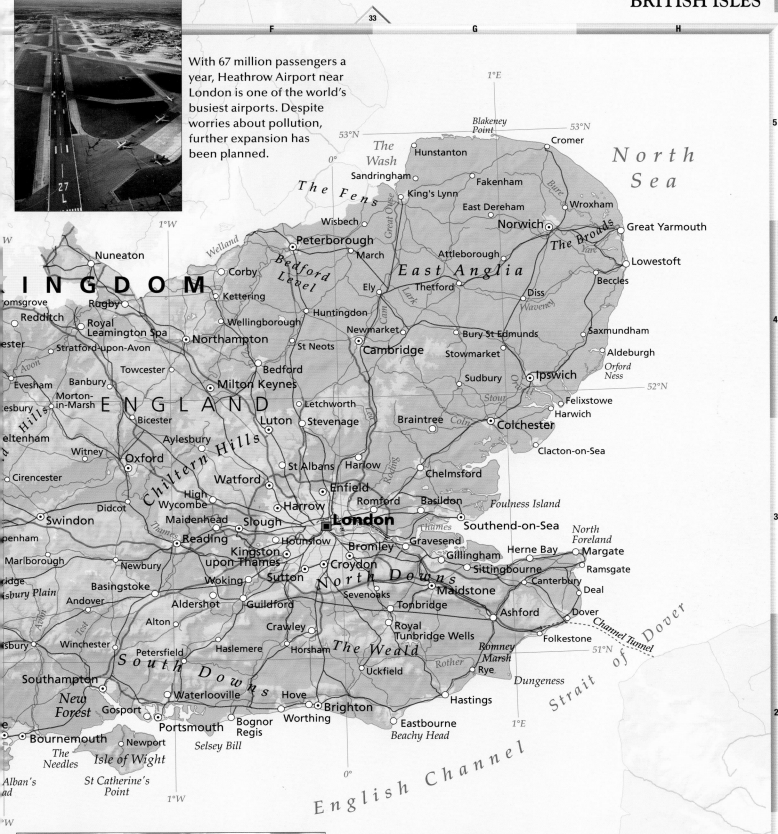

With 67 million passengers a year, Heathrow Airport near London is one of the world's busiest airports. Despite worries about pollution, further expansion has been planned.

*North Sea*

Cromer
Hunstanton
Sandringham
King's Lynn
Fakenham
East Dereham
Wroxham
*Blakeney Point*
*The Wash*
*The Fens*
Wisbech
Norwich
*The Broads*
Great Yarmouth
Peterborough
March
Attleborough
Lowestoft
*Bedford Level*
*East Anglia*
Diss
Beccles
Corby
Ely
Thetford
Kettering
Wellingborough
Huntingdon
Bury St Edmunds
Saxmundham
Nuneaton
Newmarket
Stowmarket
Aldeburgh
Rugby
Northampton
St Neots
Cambridge
*Orford Ness*
Bromsgrove
Royal Leamington Spa
Sudbury
Ipswich
Redditch
Towcester
Bedford
Felixstowe
Stratford-upon-Avon
Milton Keynes
Harwich
Evesham
Banbury
Letchworth
Braintree
Colchester
Morton-in-Marsh
*ENGLAND*
Luton
Stevenage
Bicester
Aylesbury
Clacton-on-Sea
Witney
Oxford
St Albans
Harlow
Chelmsford
Cirencester
*Chiltern Hills*
Watford
*Foulness Island*
High Wycombe
Enfield
Romford
Basildon
Cheltenham
Didcot
Harrow
Southend-on-Sea
Swindon
Maidenhead
Slough
**London**
*North Foreland*
Reading
Hounslow
Gravesend
Margate
Penham
Kingston upon Thames
Bromley
Gillingham
Herne Bay
Ramsgate
Marlborough
Newbury
Woking
Sutton
Croydon
Sittingbourne
Canterbury
Basingstoke
*North Downs*
Maidstone
Deal
Andover
Aldershot
Guildford
Sevenoaks
Dover
Alton
Tonbridge
Ashford
*Channel Tunnel*
*Strait of Dover*
Winchester
Crawley
Royal Tunbridge Wells
Folkestone
Petersfield
Haslemere
Horsham
*The Weald*
*Romney Marsh*
Southampton
*South Downs*
Uckfield
Rye
*New Forest*
Waterlooville
Hove
*Rother*
*Dungeness*
Gosport
Brighton
Hastings
Bournemouth
Portsmouth
Bognor Regis
Worthing
Eastbourne
Newport
*Selsey Bill*
*Beachy Head*
*The Needles*
*Isle of Wight*
*St Catherine's Point*

*English Channel*

UNITED KINGDOM

*Avon*
*Welland*
*Great Ouse*
*Nene*
*Cam*
*Lark*
*Waveney*
*Bure*
*Yare*
*Stour*
*Orwell*
*Colne*
*Roding*
*Thames*
*Lea*
*Test*

The White Horse at Uffington on the downs near Swindon was created 3 000 years ago and is Britain's oldest chalk carving.

## WHAT ARE SCARPS AND VALES?

Southern England was once covered by a layer of chalk, but this has been gradually worn away. Where the chalk remains it creates gentle, rounded hills that end in steep scarps overlooking flat clay vales.

# NORTHERN ENGLAND AND WALES

Northern England and Wales have many mountains and old industrial areas. The Lake District, Pennines and Cambrian Mountains form dramatic landscapes that are now preserved as National Parks. However, the rocks beneath the ground have also proved important. From the eighteenth century onwards, large quantities of coal have been brought to the surface providing the power for the Industrial Revolution. The cities that grew at that time – Cardiff, Manchester, Leeds, Newcastle and others – still dominate the region.

The mixture of lakes and rugged mountains makes the Lake District a favourite destination for tourists.

Small fields and dry stone walls create a unique landscape in the Yorkshire Dales.

*North Sea*

*Irish Sea*

SCOTLAND

Berwick-upon-Tweed
Holy Island
Farne Islands
Bamburgh
Alnwick
The Cheviot 816m
Cheviot Hills
Aln
Otterburn
Rede
Kielder Water
Morpeth
Ashington
Druridge Bay
South Shields
Newcastle upon Tyne
Gateshead
Sunderland
Washington
Hexham
Haltwhistle
Hadrian's Wall
Consett
Durham
Hartlepool
Redcar
Middlesbrough
Stockton-on-Tees
Bishop Auckland
Darlington
Catterick
Whitby
Ness Point
North York Moors
Pickering
Scarborough
Malton
The Wolds
Driffield
Flamborough Head
Bridlington
Bridlington Bay
Hornsea
Longtown
Carlisle
Wigton
Alston
Cross Fell 893m
Brough
Orton
Penrith
Helvellyn 949m
Ambleside
Windermere
Kendal
Keswick
Lake District
Scafell Pike 978m
Derwent
Workington
St Bees Head
Ravenglass
Barrow-in-Furness
Isle of Walney
Morecambe
Morecambe Bay
Lancaster
Forest of Bowland
Yorkshire Dales
Hawes
Wensleydale
Whernside 737m
Settle
Skipton
Ripon
Bedale
Northallerton
Thirsk
York
Wetherby
Harrogate
Ouse
Ure
Pennines

Isle of Man (to UK)
Point of Ayre
Ramsey
Snaefell 620m
Peel
Douglas
Port Erin
Calf of Man

2°W
3°W
5°W
5°W
55°N
55°N
54°N
54°N
54°N
54°N
1°W
0°

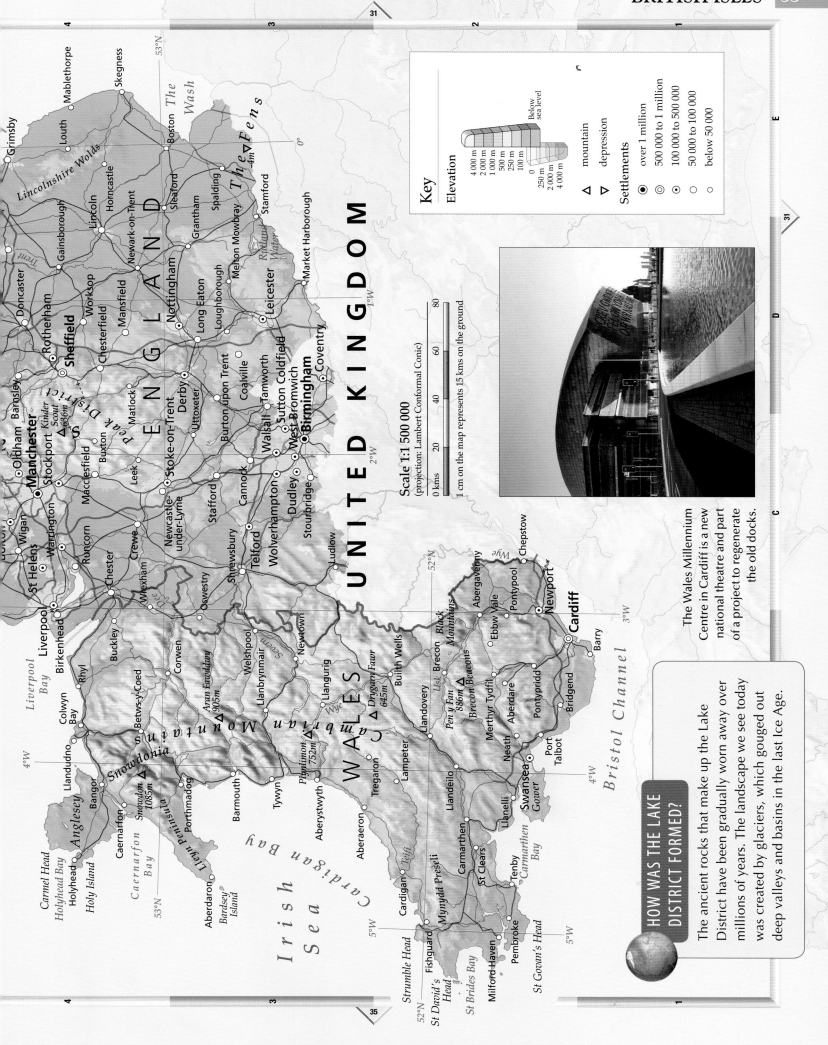

## Key

### Elevation

4 000 m
2 000 m
1 000 m
500 m
250 m
100 m
0
Below sea level

250 m
2 000 m
4 000 m

△ mountain
▽ depression

### Settlements

◉ over 1 million
◎ 500 000 to 1 million
⊙ 100 000 to 500 000
○ 50 000 to 100 000
○ below 50 000

Scale 1:1 500 000
(projection: Lambert Conformal Conic)

0 kms    20    40    60    80

1 cm on the map represents 15 kms on the ground

The Wales Millennium Centre in Cardiff is a new national theatre and part of a project to regenerate the old docks.

## HOW WAS THE LAKE DISTRICT FORMED?

The ancient rocks that make up the Lake District have been gradually worn away over millions of years. The landscape we see today was created by glaciers, which gouged out deep valleys and basins in the last Ice Age.

UNITED KINGDOM

ENGLAND

WALES

Grimsby
Mablethorpe
Louth
Skegness
Lincolnshire Wolds
Boston
The Wash
The Fens
Horncastle
Lincoln
Gainsborough
Newark-on-Trent
Sleaford
Spalding
Stamford
Grantham
Market Harborough
Melton Mowbray
Rutland Water
Doncaster
Worksop
Mansfield
Nottingham
Long Eaton
Loughborough
Leicester
Rotherham
Sheffield
Chesterfield
Derby
Coalville
Tamworth
Coventry
Manchester
Oldham
Barnsley
Stockport
Kinder Scout 636m
Peak District
Matlock
Buxton
Macclesfield
Leek
Stoke-on-Trent
Newcastle-under-Lyme
Burton upon Trent
Uttoxeter
Walsall
Sutton Coldfield
West Bromwich
Birmingham
Dudley
Stourbridge
Wolverhampton
Cannock
Stafford
Telford
Ludlow
Wigan
St Helens
Warrington
Runcorn
Crewe
Chester
Wrexham
Shrewsbury
Oswestry
Liverpool
Liverpool Bay
Birkenhead
Buckley
Newtown
Welshpool
Llanbrynmair
Llangurig
Builth Wells
Trent
Dee
Severn
Wye
Wye
Usk
Teifi
Carmel Head
Holyhead
Holyhead Bay
Holy Island
Anglesey
Caernarfon
Bangor
Colwyn Bay
Llandudno
Rhyl
Betws-y-Coed
Corwen
Aran Fawddwy 905m
Snowdonia
Snowdon 1085m
Llŷn Peninsula
Porthmadog
Caernarfon Bay
Barmouth
Cambrian Mountains
Plynlimon 752m
Aberdaron
Bardsey Island
Aberystwyth
Aberaeron
Cardigan Bay
Tywyn
Tregaron
Lampeter
Cardigan
Strumble Head
Fishguard
St David's Head
Mynydd Preseli
St Brides Bay
Milford Haven
Pembroke
St Govan's Head
Tenby
St Clears
Carmarthen
Carmarthen Bay
Llandeilo
Llandovery
Llanelli
Swansea
Gower
Neath
Port Talbot
Aberdare
Merthyr Tydfil
Pontypridd
Bridgend
Barry
Cardiff
Newport
Chepstow
Pontypool
Abergavenny
Ebbw Vale
Brecon
Black Mountains
Brecon Beacons
Pen y Fan 886m
Drygarn Fawr 645m
Bristol Channel
Irish Sea
Cardigan Bay

53°N
52°N
53°N
52°N
4°W
5°W
5°W
4°W
3°W
2°W
1°W
0°

31  3  2  1
35  3  1

# SCOTLAND

Scotland is the least populous and most northerly part of the British Isles. Most people live in Edinburgh, Glasgow and the central lowlands. Aberdeen on the east coast is a centre for the oil industry.

**ATLANTIC OCEAN**

N
W E
S

**SHETLAND ISLANDS**

ATLANTIC OCEAN

Herma Ness
1°W
Unst
Baltasound
Isbister
2°W
Yell
Brae
Ulsta
Mainland
Lerwick
North Sea
60°N
Foula
60°N
Sumburgh
1°W

Fair Isle
2°W
Scale as main map

Fair Isle
3°W
Mull Head
Westray
Sanday
Orkney Islands
Eday
Stronsay
Sule Skerry
Mainland
59°N
Stack Skerry
59°N
Hoy
Kirkwall
Pentland Firth
Duncansby Head
4°W
Dunnet Head
John o'Groats
Cape Wrath
5°W
Durness
Thurso
Loch Eriboll
Tongue
Wick
Butt of Lewis
6°W
Eye Peninsula
Lochinver
Loch Shin
Helmsdale
North Sea
Isle of Lewis
7°W
Stornoway
Reiff
Ben More Assynt 998m
Lairg
58°N
Golspie
58°N
Taransay
Ullapool
Tarbat Ness
Harris
Gairloch
Beinn Dearg 1084m
Macduff
2°W
Fraserburgh
Rodel
Loch Maree
Dingwall
Moray Firth
Elgin
Rattray Head
North Uist
Garve
3°W
Peterhead
Balivanich
Portree
Stromeferry
Inverness
Huntly
Inverurie
Benbecula
Isle of Skye
Carn Eige 1182m
Loch Ness
Monadhliath Mountains
Aviemore
Aberdeen
South Uist
Sea of the Hebrides
Cairngorm Mountains
Dee
57°N
Barra
Lochboisdale
Mallaig
S C O T L A N D
Stonehaven
7°W
Rhum
Loch Morar
Dalwhinnie
Ben Macdui 1309m
2°W
Muck
Eigg
Fort William
Montrose
Point of Ardnamurchan
Ben Nevis 1343m
Rannoch Moor
Pitlochry
Coll
Tobermory
Ben Lawers 1214m
Forfar
Arbroath
Tiree
Isle of Mull
Oban
Grampian Mountains
Loch Tay
Perth
Sidlaw Hills
Dundee
North Sea
Iona
Loch Awe
Tyndrum
Firth of Tay
Firth of Lorn
Inveraray
Ochil Hills
St Andrews
Colonsay
Stirling
Kirkcaldy
Isle of May
56°N
Loch Lomond
Forth
56°N
Dunfermline
Firth of Forth
Greenock
2°W
Clydebank
Glasgow
Edinburgh
Eyemouth
Paisley
Livingston
Lammermuir Hills
East Kilbride
Lanark
Peebles
Coldstream
Kilmarnock
Clyde
Galashiels
Tweed
Isle of Arran
Ayr
Broad Law 840m
Hawick
Cheviot Hills
Mull of Kintyre
Ailsa Craig
Girvan
Southern Uplands
Thornhill
Lockerbie
Dee
55°N
Stranraer
Castle Douglas
Dumfries
Gretna
55°N
5°W
Mull of Galloway
Solway Firth
4°W
3°W
ENGLAND

The Minch
The Little Minch
Outer Hebrides
North West Highlands
Inner Hebrides
Jura
Islay
Kintyre
North Channel

Scale 1:2 300 000
(projection: Lambert Conformal Conic)

0 kms    40    80    120

1 cm on the map represents 23 kms on the ground

# IRELAND

Rivers and lakes stretch across central Ireland while rocky mountains break up the landscape in other parts. The island is divided into two countries. Northern Ireland (part of the UK) is a relatively small area based around Belfast. The rest of the island forms a separate country, Ireland, which has Dublin as its capital.

## Key

### Elevation

4 000 m
2 000 m
1 000 m
500 m
250 m
100 m
0
250 m
2 000 m
4 000 m

Below sea level

△ mountain

### Settlements

■ ◉ over 1 million
◎ 500 000 to 1 million
⊙ 100 000 to 500 000
○ 50 000 to 100 000
○ below 50 000

A red square indicates a national capital

**Scale 1:2 400 000**
(projection: Lambert Conformal Conic)

0 kms    40    80    120

1 cm on the map represents 24 kms on the ground

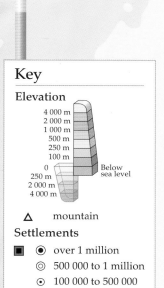

Peat bogs stretch across many parts of Ireland, blanketing a sixth of the landscape.

## WHAT ARE PEAT BOGS?

Five thousand years ago Ireland was thickly forested. As people cut down the forest, a mixture of heavy rain and half-rotted plants built up to create thick bogs. Today some peat bogs continue to be cut for fuel and fertiliser. Others have been conserved for their unique plant and insect life.

# EUROPE POLITICAL

Although Europe is one of the smallest continents, it is divided into over 40 countries and contains more than 700 million people. Many new countries were created with the break up of the Soviet Union (1989–1991). Other new countries were formed in southern Europe between 1991 and 2001 with the collapse of Yugoslavia.

## Key

■ capital city

Scale 1:25 700 000

0 kms 250  500  750  1 000

## Growth of the European Union

**Founder members 1957**
1. Netherlands
2. Belgium
3. Luxembourg
4. France
5. Germany
6. Italy

**Joined 1973**
7. Ireland
8. United Kingdom
9. Denmark

**Joined 1981**
10. Greece

**Joined 1986**
11. Portugal
12. Spain

**Joined 1995**
13. Sweden
14. Finland
15. Austria

**Joined 2004**
16. Estonia
17. Latvia
18. Lithuania
19. Poland
20. Czech Republic
21. Slovakia
22. Slovenia
23. Hungary
24. Cyprus
25. Malta

**Possible new members**
26. Croatia
27. Romania
28. Bulgaria
29. Macedonia
30. Turkey

## The European Union

Much of Europe lay in ruins after the Second World War (1939–1945) and had to be rebuilt. The leaders in France and Germany decided to work together to improve conditions and keep the peace. This was the start of the European Union. Since then the EU has grown to include 25 countries with a total population of 460 million people.

# EUROPE PHYSICAL

Europe is about 4 000 km across from north to south. In the west it faces the Atlantic Ocean. In the east the Ural Mountains form the border with Asia. The Alps are the most important mountain range as well as being the source of the river Rhine, which flows into the North Sea.

**EUROPE FACTS**

**HIGHEST MOUNTAIN:** Mount Elbrus  5 642 m

**LONGEST RIVER:** River Volga  3 531 km

**BIGGEST LAKE:** Lake Ladoga  17 700 sq km

**BIGGEST ISLAND:** Great Britain  218 595 sq km

**BIGGEST DESERT:** There are no deserts in Europe

**BIGGEST COUNTRY:** European Russia  4 294 400 sq km

**SMALLEST COUNTRY:** Vatican City  0.44 sq km

## Key

**Elevation**

4 000 m
2 000 m
1 000 m
500 m
250 m
100 m
0
250 m
2 000 m
4 000 m

Below sea level

△ mountain
⌁ volcano
▽ depression

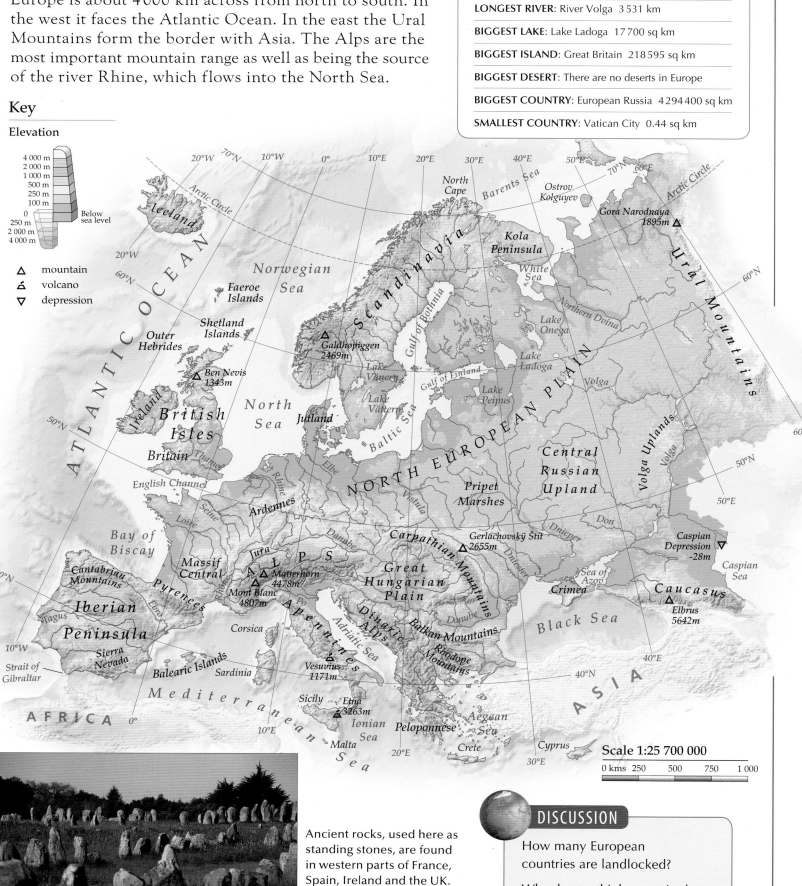

Ancient rocks, used here as standing stones, are found in western parts of France, Spain, Ireland and the UK.

Scale 1:25 700 000

0 kms  250    500    750    1 000

**DISCUSSION**

How many European countries are landlocked?

Why do you think countries keep on joining the European Union?

# EUROPE FROM THE SKY

## Environmental hotspots

**①** **Prestige oil spill, Atlantic Ocean 2002**

**②** **Forest fires, Portugal 2005**

**③** **Torrey Canyon oil spill, Scilly Isles 1967**

**④** **Avalanches, Austria 2002**

**⑤** **Acid rain damage, Czech Republic 1970s onwards**

**⑥** **Nuclear submarine dumping, Barents Sea 1950s onwards**

**⑦** **Nuclear accident, Chernobyl, Ukraine 1986**

The colours in this satellite image indicate different types of vegetation and land use. The arid areas in Spain, Turkey and the Ukraine are picked out in brown and yellow. Green represents woods and grassland. The Vatnajokull ice sheet in Iceland is light blue.

## Prestige oil spill

November 2002

Sixty four thousand tonnes of oil leaked from the wreck of the Prestige in 2002, killing wildlife and polluting beaches in Spain, Portugal and France.

## Europe at night

Towns and cities show up clearly on this night-time image. London, Paris, Moscow and Madrid appear as a blaze of light. The flares from oil rigs can be seen in the North Sea.

## Flooding in Carlisle

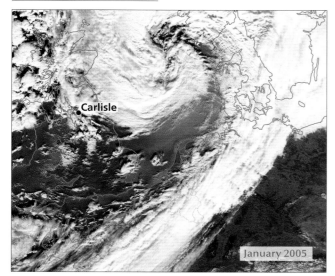

January 2005

The Atlantic depression that swept across Britain and northwest Europe in January 2005 caused the worst flooding for a century in Carlisle and other parts of Cumbria. The spiral of clouds in this photograph shows the position of weather fronts.

## Mount Etna eruption

October 2002

*Mediterranean Sea*

*Sicily*

When Mount Etna erupted, the wind carried a plume of smoke and ash hundreds of kilometres across the eastern Mediterranean.

## Amsterdam city centre

North Sea canal

Cathedral

Central station

Docks

Theatre

Line of old city wall

Rijksmuseum

Vondel Park

2005

Founded in the thirteenth century, Amsterdam has grown from being a small port to a modern capital city. The pattern of streets and canals around the historic core, along with individual buildings, shows up clearly from the air.

# NORTHERN EUROPE

Northern Europe is the coldest and emptiest part of the continent. There are icy mountains and deep fjords along the coast of Norway. Sweden and Finland are much flatter with many forests and lakes. The Baltic States (Estonia, Latvia and Lithuania) have more land used for growing crops.

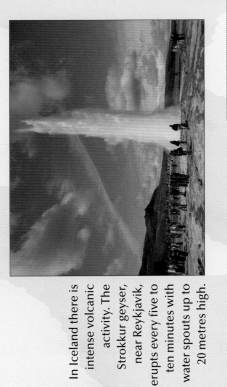

In Iceland there is intense volcanic activity. The Strokkur geyser, near Reykjavik, erupts every five to ten minutes with water spouts up to 20 metres high.

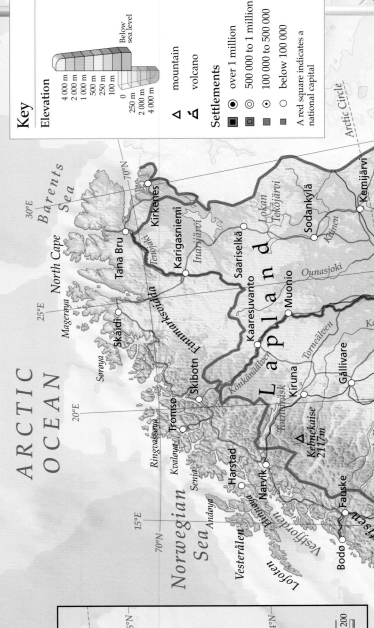

## Key

### Elevation

4 000 m
2 000 m
1 000 m
500 m
250 m
100 m
0
250 m
2 000 m
4 000 m

Below sea level

△ mountain
🌋 volcano

### Settlements

⊙ over 1 million
◎ 500 000 to 1 million
⊙ 100 000 to 500 000
○ below 100 000

■ A red square indicates a national capital

## ICELAND inset

ICELAND

Scale 1:6 100 000

0 kms 100 200

ATLANTIC OCEAN

Greenland Sea

Ísafjördhur
Raufarhöfn
Grímsey
Akureyri
Saudhárkrókur
Stykkishólmur
**ICELAND**
Djúpivogur
Vatnajökull
Hvannadalshnúkur 2119m
Borgarnes
Selfoss
Myrdalsjökull
Hofsjökull
Thjórsá
**Reykjavik**
Keflavik
Heimaey
Surtsey
Faxaflói
Breidhafjördhur
Húnaflói
Arctic Circle

66°N
64°N
24°W 22°W 20°W 18°W 16°W 14°W

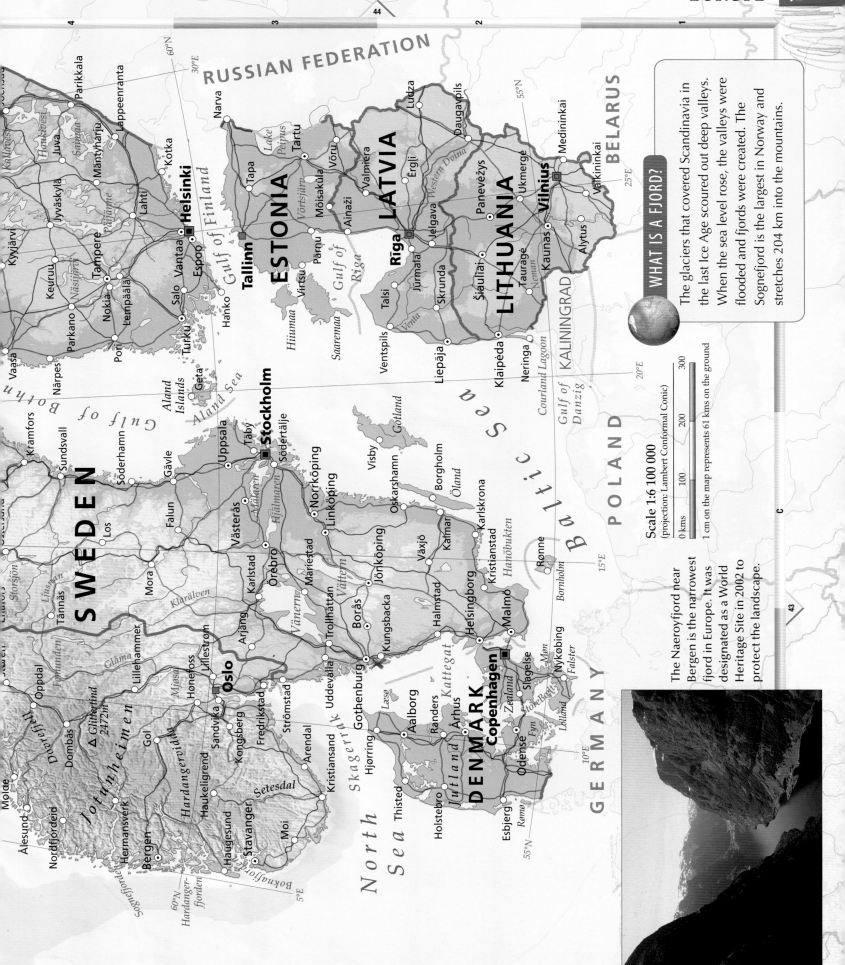

RUSSIAN FEDERATION

BELARUS

## SWEDEN

## FINLAND

### ESTONIA

### LATVIA

### LITHUANIA

### DENMARK

### POLAND

### GERMANY

### KALININGRAD

Narva
Parikkala
Lappeenranta
Kylläres
Hankoesi
Juva
Mäntyharju
Kotka
Kyyjärvi
Keuruu
Jyväskylä
Lahti
**Helsinki**
Tampere
Nokia
Lempäälä
Vantaa
Espoo
Parkano
Pori
Salo
Turku
Hanko
Vaasa
Närpes

Lake Peipus
Tartu
Tapa
Võru
Valmiera
Ludza
Daugavpils
Medininkai
Valkininkai
Vilnius
Ukmergė
Panevėžys
Jelgava
Ėrgli
Mõisaküla
Pärnu
Ainaži
Virtsu
**Tallinn**
**Rīga**
Jūrmala
Skrunda
Talsi
Šiauliai
Taurage
Kaunas
Alytus
Ventspils
Liepāja
Klaipėda
Neringa
Hiiumaa
Saaremaa
Gulf of Riga
Vörtsjärv
Courland Lagoon
Western Dvina
Venta
Neman

Gulf of Finland
Gulf of Danzig

Geta
Åland Islands
Åland Sea
Aland Sea
**Stockholm**
Uppsala
Täby
Södertälje
Norrköping
Linköping
Visby
Gotland
Borgholm
Öland
Oskarshamn
Kalmar
Karlskrona
Ronne
Bornholm

Kramfors
Sundsvall
Söderhamn
Gävle
Falun
Los
Mora
Västerås
Örebro
Karlstad
Arjäng
Mariestad
Trollhättan
Uddevalla
Gothenburg
Borås
Kungsbacka
Jönköping
Växjö
Halmstad
Helsingborg
Kristianstad
Hanöbukten
Malmö
Helsingborg

Storsjön
Mälaren
Hjälmaren
Vänern
Vättern
Klarälven

Oppdal
Dombås
Lillehammer
Honefoss
Lillestrøm
**Oslo**
Sandvika
Gol
Kongsberg
Fredrikstad
Strömstad
Arendal
Kristiansand
Moi
Stavanger
Haugesund
Haukeligrend
Sandnes
Molde
Ålesund
Nordfjordeid
Hermansverk
Bergen
Dovrefjell
Jotunheimen
△ Glittertind 2472m
Hardangervidda
Setesdal
Boknafjord
Hardanger-fjorden
Sognefjord
Glåma
Mjøsa

Hjørring
Aalborg
Randers
Århus
Odense
Esbjerg
Holstebro
Thisted
**Copenhagen**
Slagelse
StoreBælt
Zealand
Fyn
Mon
Nykobing
Falster
Lolland
Rømo
Jutland
Kattegat
Læsø
Skagerrak

North Sea

Baltic Sea

Gulf of Bothnia

### WHAT IS A FJORD?

The glaciers that covered Scandinavia in the last Ice Age scoured out deep valleys. When the sea level rose, the valleys were flooded and fjords were created. The Sognefjord is the largest in Norway and stretches 204 km into the mountains.

The Naeroyfjord near Bergen is the narrowest fjord in Europe. It was designated as a World Heritage Site in 2002 to protect the landscape.

### Scale 1:6 100 000
(projection: Lambert Conformal Conic)

0 kms   100   200   300

1 cm on the map represents 61 kms on the ground

60°N
55°N
55°N
60°E
30°E
25°E
20°E
15°E
10°E
5°E

# WESTERN EUROPE

Western Europe faces the Atlantic Ocean. Winds bring moist air from the southwest to the rocky coasts of Britain, Ireland, France, Spain and Portugal. In the past, mariners from these seafaring nations set out to explore the world in sailing ships. Today trade still dominates the economy of western Europe, which is one of the most prosperous areas in the world.

The dramatic limestone scenery of the Dolomites in northern Italy attracts tourists and skiers. Scientists believe recent rock falls are partly the result of abnormal heating and cooling linked to climate change.

## Key

### Elevation

4 000 m
2 000 m
1 000 m
500 m
250 m
100 m
0
250 m
2 000 m
4 000 m

Below sea level

△ mountain

### Settlements

| | | |
|---|---|---|
| ■ | ⊙ | over 1 million |
| ▣ | ◎ | 500 000 to 1 million |
| ▪ | ⊙ | 100 000 to 500 000 |
| ▪ | | below 100 000 |

A red square indicates a national capital

⌂ volcano

### Map labels

5°W
0°
10°W
55°N
Nort
10°W
50°N
English Channel
N
W  E
S
10°W
45°N
10°W
40°N
10°W
5°W
0°

ATLANTIC OCEAN

Grampians
Aberdeen
Dundee
Glasgow  Edinburgh
UNITED KINGDOM
Belfast
Isle of Man (to UK)
Newcastle upon Tyne
IRELAND
Leeds
Manchester
Dublin
Liverpool  Sheffield
Nottingham
Cork
Birmingham
Norw
Oxford
Cardiff  London
Southampton  Brighton
Plymouth
Channel Islands (to UK)
le Havre
Lil
Rouer
Seine
Paris
Rennes
Orlé
Loire
St-Nazaire  Nantes  Tours
FRA
Limoges
Mass
Cent
Bay of Biscay
Bordeaux
Garonne
A Coruña
Gijón
Santander
Toulo
Vigo
Cordillera Cantábrica
Bilbao
León
Pyrenees
ANDO
Burgos
Oporto
Valladolid
Ebro
Barcelo
Salamanca
Zaragoza
Coimbra
Tarragon
Madrid
PORTUGAL
Tagus
SPAIN
Mallo
Lisbon
Palma de Mallorca
Badajoz
Valencia
Ibiza
Balea
Islan
Córdoba
Murcia
Seville
Granada
Cartagena
Me
Cádiz
Málaga
Gibraltar (to UK)

Scale 1:9 600 000
(projection: Lambert Conformal Conic)

0 kms    200    400    600

1 cm on the map represents 96 kms on the ground

Rotterdam, at the mouth of the river Rhine, is Europe's largest port. It handles oil, coal, metal ore and containers from all around the world.

Italy, France and Spain are the world's biggest wine producers. This farmer in Sicily is tending the vines on his farm.

## WHAT IS THE NORTH ATLANTIC DRIFT?

The ocean current that brings warmth from the Caribbean to western Europe is known as the North Atlantic Drift. It carries as much energy as 1 million power stations. Without this current, winters in western Europe could be 10 degrees colder and the sea would freeze in many places.

# EASTERN EUROPE

Romania, Poland, Ukraine and the Russian Federation are the largest countries in eastern Europe. In Russia two great rivers, the Don and the Volga, thread their way to the sea past fields and factories. In southeast Europe, the river Danube links four capital cities on its journey from the edge of the Alps to the Black Sea. Many parts of eastern Europe have a continental climate with marked differences between summer and winter temperatures.

Many countries in eastern Europe have broken away from the Russian Federation. These crowds gathered in Kiev in 2004 to challenge the results of an election.

One of the world's most beautiful Gothic gateways, the Charles Bridge in Prague, attracts many tourists. It was built across the river Vltava in the fourteenth century by King Charles IV to link the old town with the castle opposite.

RUSSIAN FEDERATION

Ural Mountains

Kara Sea

Novaya Zemlya

Ostrov Vaygach

Barents Sea

Ostrov Kolguyev

Pechora

Naryan-Mar

Vorkuta

Ukhta

Perm'

Syktyvkar

Kirov

Severnaya Dvina

Archangel

Vologda

White Sea

Onega

Petrozavodsk

Cherepovets

Kola Peninsula

Lake Onega

Murmansk

Lake Ladoga

Novgorod

NORWAY

Arctic Circle

FINLAND

Saint Petersburg

Lake Peipus

ESTONIA

Arctic Circle

WHAT ARE THE STEPPES?

The grasslands that stretch across southern parts of the Russian Federation and the Ukraine are known as the steppes. The flat land and thick black soil that is found here are ideal for farming wheat. As a result the steppes are known as the bread basket of Europe.

## Key

### Elevation

4 000 m
2 000 m
1 000 m
500 m
250 m
100 m
0
250 m
2 000 m
4 000 m
Below sea level

△ mountain

### Settlements

■ over 1 million
▣ 500 000 to 1 million
▪ 100 000 to 500 000
○ below 100 000

A red square indicates a national capital

Scale 1:13 600 000
(projection: Lambert Conformal Conic)

0 kms    200    400    600    800

1 cm on the map represents 136 kms on the ground

### Map labels

Orsk
Orenburg
Samara
Ul'yanovsk
Tol'yatti
Balakovo
Saratov
Penza
Novgorod
Tambov
Ryazan'
Voronezh
Kamyshin
Oral
Tula
Kursk
Orël
Don
Syeverodonets'k
Kharkiv
Dnipropetrovs'k
Donets'k
Volgograd
Volgodonsk
Rostov-na-Donu
Volga
Astrakhan'
Caspian Depression
Caspian Sea
Grozny
Pyatigorsk
△ Elbrus 5642 m
Krasnodar
Caucasus
GEORGIA
AZERBAIJAN
45°E
50°E
45°N

KAZAKHSTAN

Kiev
Kirovohrad
Mariupol'
Melitopol'
Kerch
Sochi
Chernihiv
Sumy
Cherkasy
UKRAINE
Zhytomyr
Vinnytsya
Odesa
Simferopol'
Sevastopol'
Black Sea
40°E
35°E

Vitsyebsk
Mahilyow
Homyel'
Minsk
BELARUS
Polatsk
Brest
Pripet Marshes
Dnieper
Chişinău
MOLDOVA
Constanţa
Burgas
Istanbul
TURKEY
40°N
30°E

Kaliningrad
Warsaw
POLAND
Białystok
Lublin
L'viv
Košice
Cluj-Napoca
Braşov
Pleven
Plovdiv
BULGARIA
Sofia
Bucharest
ROMANIA
Carpathian Mountains
Danube
Piteşti
Pécs
Timişoara
Thessaloniki
35°E

Szczecin
Gdańsk
Poznań
Łódź
Wrocław
Katowice
Kraków
Olomouc
CZECH REPUBLIC
Prague
SLOVAKIA
Bratislava
Budapest
HUNGARY
AUSTRIA
SLOVENIA
Zagreb
CROATIA
Split
Osijek
BOSNIA & HERZEGOVINA
Sarajevo
Belgrade
SERBIA & MONTENEGRO (YUGOSLAVIA)
Priština
Skopje
MACEDONIA
Tirana
ALBANIA
Adriatic Sea
Ionian Islands
Ionian Sea
15°E
45°N
40°N
35°N
20°E
25°E

GERMANY
50°N

GREECE
Larisa
Athens
Pátra
Cyclades
Dodecanese
Irákleio
Crete
Mediterranean Sea

TURKISH REPUBLIC OF NORTHERN CYPRUS
(recognised only by Turkey)
Nicosia
CYPRUS
Limassol
35°N
35°E

Caspian Sea
45°N

# AFRICA POLITICAL

There are 54 countries in Africa. Many African countries gained independence from Europe in the 1960s and 1970s. Although there have been frequent disputes since then, there have been few changes to the borders which were imposed at the time by colonial rulers.

## New countries

In 1950, there were just four independent countries in Africa, but now all of the nations on the mainland are self-governing.

**Key**

■ capital city

Living conditions and human development are priorities for many African countries. In Mozambique, after 16 years of conflict, the government is concentrating on improving the school system.

Scale 1:46 000 000

0 kms    500    1 000    1 500

# AFRICA PHYSICAL

Africa is the second largest continent. It stretches from the Mediterranean Sea to the Cape of Good Hope. Nearly all of Africa lies in the Tropics. Deserts, rainforests and grasslands make up much of the landscape. In the south and east of the continent there are high plains where the sources of many of Africa's famous rivers are found.

## AFRICA FACTS

**HIGHEST MOUNTAIN:** Mount Kilimanjaro 5 895 m

**LONGEST RIVER:** River Nile 6 671 km

**BIGGEST LAKE:** Lake Victoria 69 500 sq km

**BIGGEST ISLAND:** Madagascar 581 540 sq km

**BIGGEST DESERT:** Sahara desert 9 000 000 sq km

**BIGGEST COUNTRY:** Sudan 2 505 810 sq km

**SMALLEST COUNTRY:** Seychelles 455 sq km

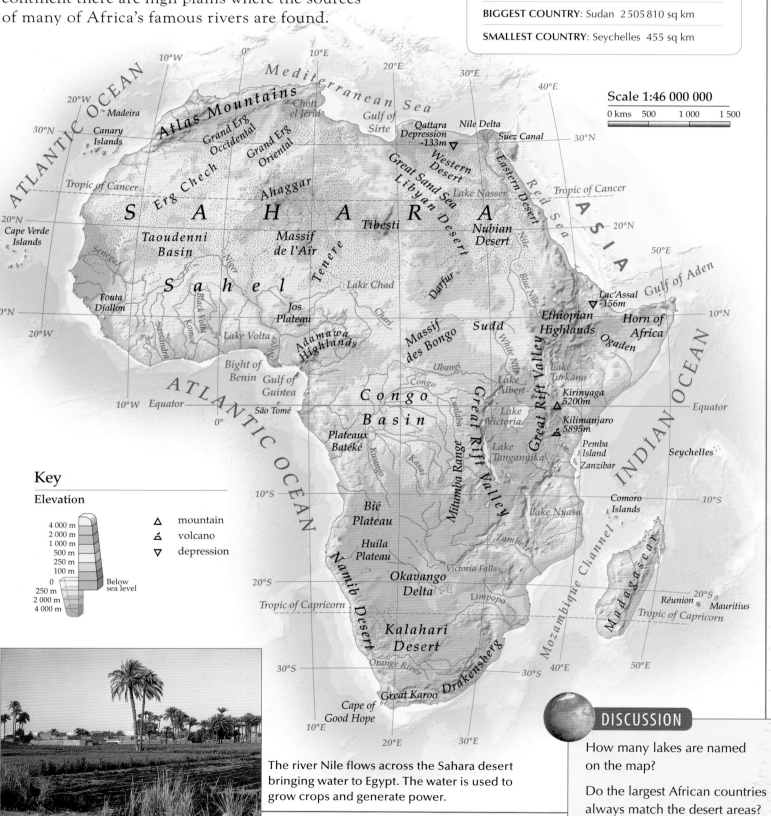

Scale 1:46 000 000

0 kms 500 1 000 1 500

## Key

### Elevation

4 000 m
2 000 m
1 000 m
500 m
250 m
100 m
0
250 m
2 000 m
4 000 m

Below sea level

△ mountain
⌂ volcano
▽ depression

The river Nile flows across the Sahara desert bringing water to Egypt. The water is used to grow crops and generate power.

## DISCUSSION

How many lakes are named on the map?

Do the largest African countries always match the desert areas?

# AFRICA FROM THE SKY

El Kelaa, Morocco •

Egypt/Sudan border

*Lake Chad*

Equator

## Environmental hotspots

**1** Oil spills, Niger delta ongoing

**2** Landmines, Angola ongoing

**3** Drought, Zimbabwe, 2002 ongoing

**4** Floods, Mozambique 2000, 2001

**5** Drought, Ethiopia, 1984 ongoing

**6** Melting glaciers, Kilimanjaro, Tanzania ongoing

**7** Retreating mangrove forests, Tanzania ongoing

The Sahara desert stretches across northern Africa as a yellow band in this satellite image. The orange area in southwest Africa marks the Kalahari desert. The rainforests and grasslands either side of the Equator show up in green. You can even trace the course of the river Nile as it threads its way to the Mediterranean Sea.

## Africa at night

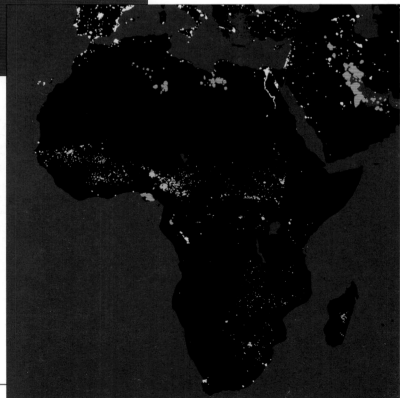

In this colour-coded image, city lights are shown in yellow, oil flares in red and forest fires in purple. Note how few lights there are in Africa compared with southern Europe (at the top of the image).

## Flooding in Mozambique

February 2000

The cyclones, which hit Mozambique in 2000 and 2001, destroyed crops and made half a million people homeless.

## Rose cultivation

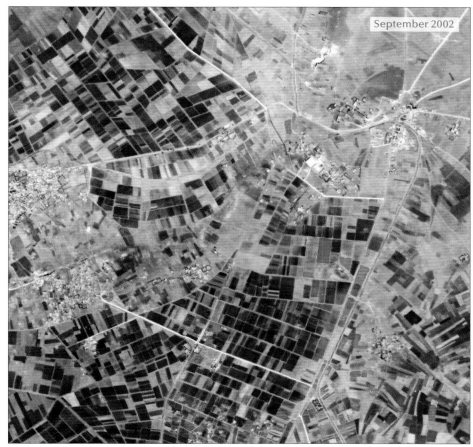

September 2002

The El Kelaa region of Morocco is famous for rose water. In this photograph, the rose fields are shown in green and red. You can see the settlements in pale blue.

## Lake Chad

1968

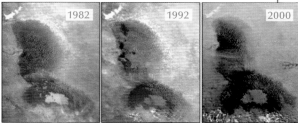

1982  1992  2000

Lake Chad lies in an internal drainage basin. Satellite images record how the lake has shrivelled over the last few decades.

## Fields in the desert

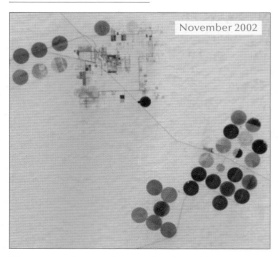

November 2002

These circular fields near the Egypt-Sudan border are irrigated with underground water. The water has taken thousands of years to accumulate, but is unlikely to last beyond 2050 if people continue to use the same amounts as they do at the moment.

## Sandstorm over Africa

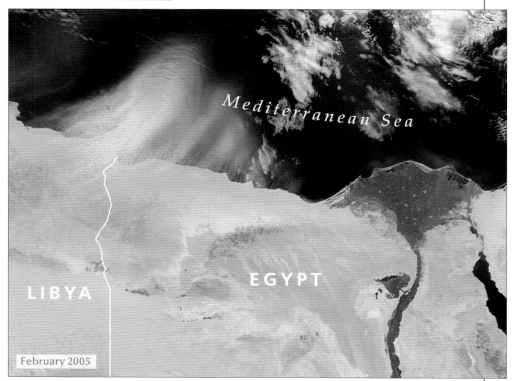

Mediterranean Sea

LIBYA

EGYPT

February 2005

Strong winds in the Sahara desert sometimes whip up the sand and blow it into the sea. Note the Nile delta and Red Sea on the eastern side of this image.

# NORTH AFRICA

The world's largest desert, the Sahara, stretches nearly 5 000 km across North Africa from the Atlantic Ocean to the Red Sea. There are few permanent settlements in this parched landscape. To the south, there are grasslands. To the north, along the Mediterranean Sea, a narrow strip of land also receives enough rain to grow crops.

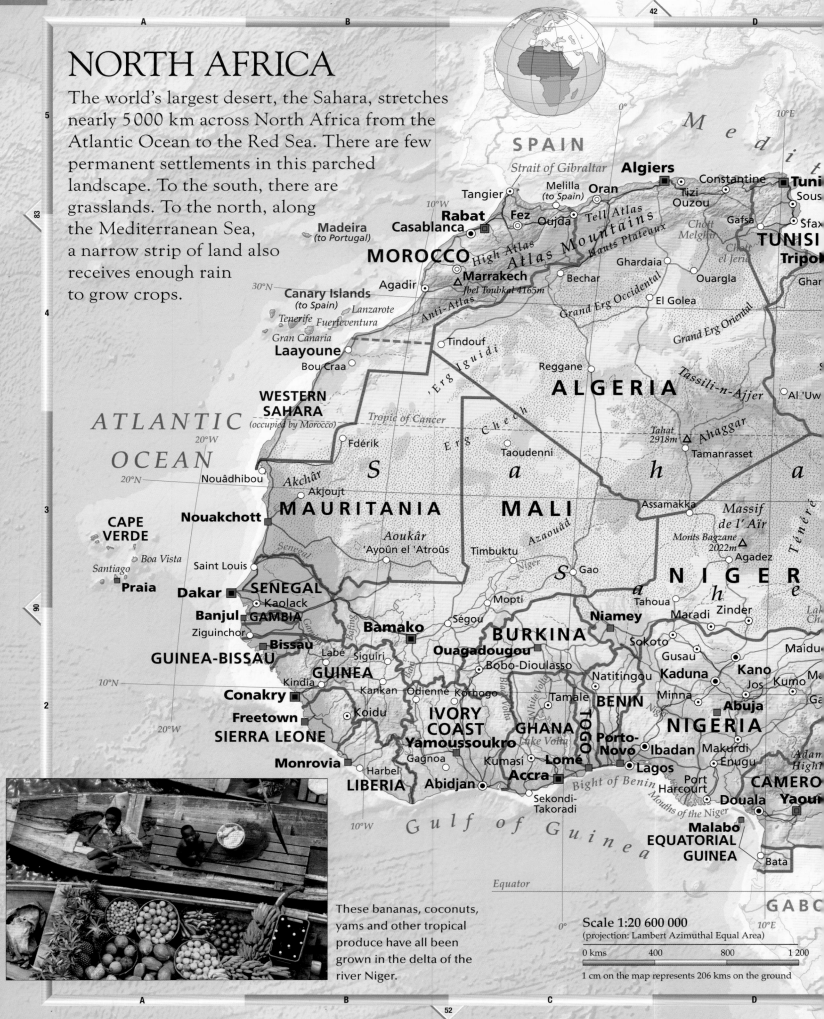

**SPAIN**

*Strait of Gibraltar*

Tangier
Melilla *(to Spain)*
**Algiers**
Constantine
**Tuni**
Tizi Ouzou
Sous

Oran

**Rabat**
Fez
Oujda
*Tell Atlas*
Gafsa
Sfax

**Casablanca**
*Madeira (to Portugal)*
*Atlas Mountains*
*Chott Melghir*

**MOROCCO**
*High Atlas*
*Hauts Plateaux*
**TUNISI**

Agadir
△ *Jbel Toubkal 4165m*
Ghardaia
*Chott el Jerid*
**Tripol**

*30°N*
**Canary Islands** *(to Spain)*
*Anti-Atlas*
Bechar
Ouargla
Ghar

*Tenerife* *Lanzarote*
*Fuerteventura*
*Grand Erg Occidental*
El Golea

*Gran Canaria*
Tindouf
*Grand Erg Oriental*

**Laayoune**
*'Erg Iguidi*
Reggane
*Tassili-n-Ajjer*

Bou Craa
**ALGERIA**
Al 'Uw

**WESTERN SAHARA**
*(occupied by Morocco)*
*Tropic of Cancer*
*Erg Chech*
Tahat 2918m △ △ *Ahaggar*

Fdérik
Taoudenni
Tamanrasset

**ATLANTIC**
*20°W*
*a*

**OCEAN**
Nouâdhibou
*Akchâr*
*S*
*a*
*h*

*20°N*
Akjoujt
Assamakka
*Massif de l'Aïr*

**CAPE VERDE**
**MAURITANIA**
**MALI**
*Monts Bagzane 2022m* △

*Boa Vista*
Nouakchott
*Aoukâr*
Agadez
*Ténéré*

*Santiago*
*Senegal*
'Ayoûn el 'Atroûs
Timbuktu
*Azaouâd*

**Praia**
Saint Louis
*Niger*
Gao
**NIGER**

**Dakar**
**SENEGAL**
*S*
*h*

Kaolack
Mopti
Tahoua
Zinder

**Banjul**
**GAMBIA**
**Bamako**
Ségou
*a*
Maradi

Ziguinchor
*Baoule*
**BURKINA**
Sokoto

**Bissau**
Labé Siguiri
**Ouagadougou**
Gusau
**Kano**

**GUINEA-BISSAU**
Bobo-Dioulasso
Natitingou
**Kaduna**
Kumo

**GUINEA**
Kindia
Kankan
Odienné Korhogo
Tamale
**BENIN**
Minna
Maidu

**Conakry**
Koidu
*White Volta*
**Ibadan**
**Abuja**

**Freetown**
Koidu
**IVORY COAST**
**GHANA**
**TOGO**
**NIGERIA**

**SIERRA LEONE**
**Yamoussoukro**
Kumasi
**Porto-Novo**
Makurdi

**Monrovia**
Gagnoa
*Lake Volta*
**Lomé**
**Ibadan**
Enugu

Harbel
Sekondi-Takoradi
**Accra**
**Lagos**
Port Harcourt
**CAMERO**

**LIBERIA**
Abidjan
*Bight of Benin*
*Mouths of the Niger*
**Douala**
**Yaou**

*Gulf of Guinea*
**Malabo**
**EQUATORIAL GUINEA**
Bata

*Equator*
**GAB**

These bananas, coconuts, yams and other tropical produce have all been grown in the delta of the river Niger.

**Scale 1:20 600 000**
(projection: Lambert Azimuthal Equal Area)

| 0 kms | 400 | 800 | 1 200 |

1 cm on the map represents 206 kms on the ground

An oasis can vary from being just a few trees in the desert to a great city on an old trading route.

## WHAT IS AN OASIS?

At some places in a desert, water that is trapped in underground rocks comes out on the surface. This creates an oasis. By moving from one oasis to another, nomads and travellers are able to survive in the harsh desert climate.

**N** W E S

**CYPRUS**

*20°E*
*30°E*

*ran ean Sea*

Al Bayda'
Tobruk
sratah
*ulf of Sirte*
**Benghazi**
**Alexandria**
*Nile Delta*
**Port Said**
**ISRAEL**
**JORDAN**
*Suez Canal*
*Qattara Depression*
**El Giza**
Suez
**Cairo**
*Sinai*
*30°N*
Waddan
Jalu
*Great Sand Sea*
El Minya
△ *Gebel Musa 2285m*

**LIBYA**
*Libyan Desert*
**EGYPT**
El Kharga
Asyut
Luxor

*Ramlat Rabyanah*
Al Khufrah
Aswan
*40°E*
*Tropic of Cancer*

△ *Pic Bette 2286m*
*Lake Nasser*

*Tibesti*
*r*
Jabal al 'Uwaynāt 1907m △ *a*
Akasha
*Nubian Desert*
*20°N*

Zouar

△ *Emi Koussi 3415m*
El'Atrun
**SAUDI ARABIA**

Faya
*Ennedi*
Atbara
Port Sudan
**YEMEN**
*50°E*

**HAD**
*Darfur*
Omdurman
**Khartoum**
Wad Medani
**ERITREA**
Kassala
**Asmara**
*Red Sea*

Abéché
El Fasher
**SUDAN**
Gedaref
*Gulf of Aden*

djamena
El Obeid
Gonder
Aseb
*Lac' Assal -156m* ▽

Nyala
*Blue Nile*
Bahir Dar
Dese
**DJIBOUTI**
*Djibouti*
Berbera
△ *Shimbiris 2407m*
*Raas Xaafuun*

indou
Sarh
Birao
*Bahr Aouk*
Malakal
*Lake Tana*
*Abuye Meda 4000m* △
Dire Dawa
Hargeysa
**SOMALIA**
*10°N*

*Chari*
*White Nile*
*Ethiopian*
**Addis Ababa**
*Great Rift Valley*
Garoowe

ouar
**CENTRAL**
Wau
*Sudd*
*Highlands*
Jima
**ETHIOPIA**
*Ogaden*
*Shebeli*

bérati
**AFRICAN REPUBLIC**
Bambari
Obo
*Bomu*
Juba
Negele
Beledweyne

**Bangui**
*Oubangui*
*Kotto*
*White Nile*
*Lake Turkana*

**DEM. REP. CONGO**
**UGANDA**
*30°E*
*20°E*

*GO*
*uator*
**KENYA**
Marka
*Juba*
**Mogadishu**

*Equator*
*Equator*

Kismaayo
*50°E*
*40°E*
**INDIAN OCEAN**

## Key

**Elevation**

4 000 m
2 000 m
1 000 m
500 m
250 m
100 m
0
Below sea level
250 m
2 000 m
4 000 m

**Settlements**

■ ⊙ over 1 million
▣ ◎ 500 000 to 1 million
▪ ⊙ 100 000 to 500 000
▪ ○ below 100 000

A red square indicates a national capital

△ mountain     ▽ depression

# SOUTHERN AFRICA

Much of southern Africa is 1 000 metres or more above sea level. It is famous for the wild animals that roam across the grasslands. Great rivers such as the Orange and Zambezi drain the uplands. There are valuable reserves of gold, copper, diamonds and other minerals across the region. However, most of the wealth goes to other countries and southern Africa remains one of the poorest parts of the world.

The Victoria Falls on the river Zambesi are the largest curtain of water in the world (1.7 km wide) and a UNESCO World Heritage Site.

The Great Rift Valley cuts across Tanzania with steep slopes along the sides and a valley up to 60 km wide.

**Scale 1:18 500 000**
(projection: Lambert Azimuthal Equal Area)

| 0 kms | 400 | 800 | 1 200 |

1 cm on the map represents 185 kms on the ground

## Key

### Elevation

4 000 m
2 000 m
1 000 m
500 m
250 m
100 m
0
250 m
2 000 m
4 000 m
Below sea level

### Settlements

| ■ | ⊙ | over 1 million |
| ▣ | ◎ | 500 000 to 1 million |
| ▦ | ⊙ | 100 000 to 500 000 |
| ▪ | ○ | below 100 000 |

A red square indicates a national capital

△ mountain   ▽ depression

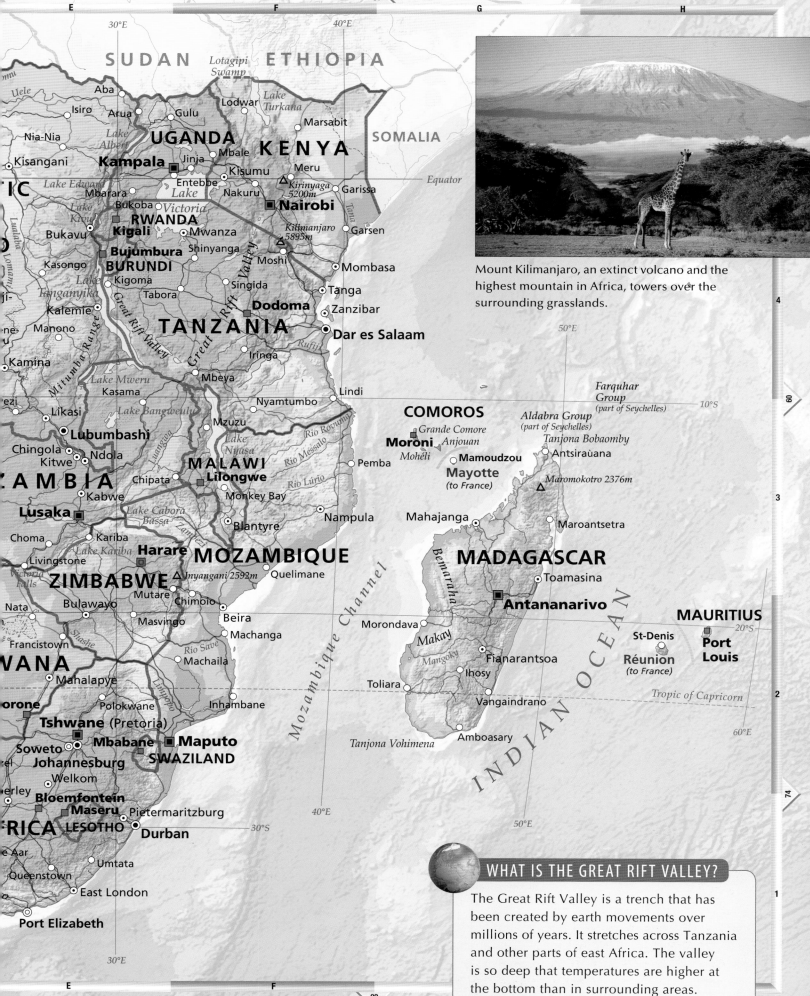

Mount Kilimanjaro, an extinct volcano and the highest mountain in Africa, towers over the surrounding grasslands.

SUDAN
ETHIOPIA
Lotagipi Swamp
Uele
Umu
Aba
Isiro
Nia-Nia
Arua
Gulu
Lodwar
Lake Turkana
SOMALIA
Kisangani
Lake Albert
UGANDA
Kampala
Jinja
Mbale
KENYA
Marsabit
Meru
Kisumu
Entebbe
Lake Victoria
Nakuru
Kirinyaga 5200m
Garissa
Equator
Mbarara
Bukoba
Nairobi
Tana
RWANDA
Lake Kivu
Kigali
Mwanza
Garsen
Bukavu
Shinyanga
Kilimanjaro 5895m
Kasongo
BURUNDI
Bujumbura
Kigoma
Singida
Moshi
Lualaba
Lomami
Lake Tanganyika
Tabora
Mombasa
Kalemie
TANZANIA
Dodoma
Tanga
Manono
Zanzibar
Kamina
Great Rift Valley
Mitumba Range
Iringa
Rufiji
Dar es Salaam
Mbeya
Lake Mweru
Kasama
Nyamtumbo
Lindi
Likasi
Lake Bangweulu
Mzuzu
COMOROS
Farquhar Group (part of Seychelles)
Lubumbashi
Rio Rovuma
Grande Comore
Aldabra Group (part of Seychelles)
Chingola
Kitwe
Ndola
MALAWI
Lake Nyasa
Rio Messalo
Moroni
Anjouan
Tanjona Bobaomby
Antsiraùana
ZAMBIA
Chipata
Lilongwe
Rio Lúrio
Mohéli
Mamoudzou
Maromokotro 2376m
Kabwe
Monkey Bay
Pemba
Mayotte (to France)
Lusaka
Luangwa
Nampula
Mahajanga
Maroantsetra
Choma
Kariba
Lake Cabora Bassa
Blantyre
Zambezi
Lake Kariba
Harare
MOZAMBIQUE
MADAGASCAR
Livingstone
Victoria Falls
ZIMBABWE
Inyangani 2592m
Quelimane
Bemaraha
Toamasina
Nata
Bulawayo
Mutare
Chimoio
Antananarivo
MAURITIUS
Francistown
Shashe
Masvingo
Beira
Machanga
Morondava
St-Denis
Port Louis
Rio Save
Makay
Fianarantsoa
Réunion (to France)
BOTSWANA
Machaila
Mangoky
Ihosy
Mahalapye
Mozambique Channel
Toliara
Vangaindrano
Gaborone
Polokwane
Inhambane
Limpopo
INDIAN OCEAN
Tropic of Capricorn
Amboasary
Tanjona Vohimena
Tshwane (Pretoria)
Soweto
Mbabane
Maputo
Johannesburg
SWAZILAND
Welkom
AFRICA
Bloemfontein
Maseru
Pietermaritzburg
LESOTHO
Durban
de Aar
Umtata
Queenstown
East London
Port Elizabeth

30°E  40°E  50°E  60°E  10°S  20°S  30°S

## WHAT IS THE GREAT RIFT VALLEY?

The Great Rift Valley is a trench that has been created by earth movements over millions of years. It stretches across Tanzania and other parts of east Africa. The valley is so deep that temperatures are higher at the bottom than in surrounding areas.

# ASIA POLITICAL

Home to many ancient civilisations, Asia is divided into 49 countries. Although the Russian Federation is biggest in terms of area, India, China, Pakistan, Indonesia and Bangladesh all have larger populations. There are many border disputes and the Middle East (the area to the south of Turkey) has seen decades of conflict.

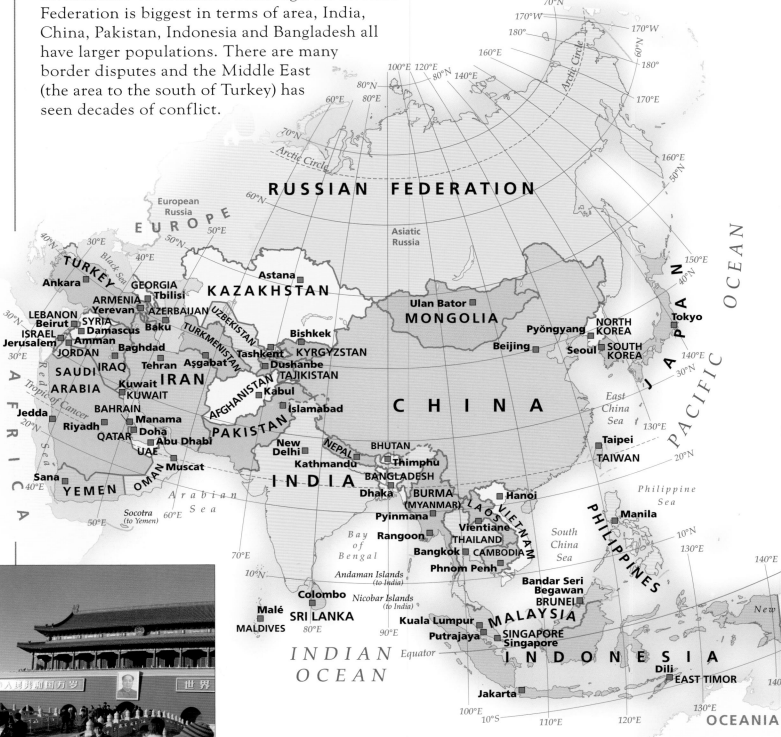

RUSSIAN FEDERATION

European Russia

EUROPE

Asiatic Russia

Arctic Circle

TURKEY
Ankara
GEORGIA
Tbilisi
ARMENIA
Yerevan
AZERBAIJAN
Baku
Black Sea

KAZAKHSTAN
Astana

MONGOLIA
Ulan Bator

Pyŏngyang
NORTH KOREA
Beijing
Seoul
SOUTH KOREA

Tokyo

JAPAN

PACIFIC OCEAN

LEBANON
Beirut
SYRIA
Damascus
ISRAEL
Jerusalem
Amman
JORDAN
Baghdad
IRAQ
Tehran
Kuwait
KUWAIT
IRAN
BAHRAIN
Manama
Riyadh
Doha
QATAR
Abu Dhabi
UAE
SAUDI ARABIA

UZBEKISTAN
Tashkent
TURKMENISTAN
Aşgabat
Bishkek
KYRGYZSTAN
Dushanbe
TAJIKISTAN
AFGHANISTAN
Kabul
Islamabad
PAKISTAN

CHINA

East China Sea

Taipei
TAIWAN

Jedda
Tropic of Cancer
Red Sea
Sana
YEMEN
OMAN
Muscat
Socotra (to Yemen)

Arabian Sea

New Delhi
NEPAL
Kathmandu
BHUTAN
Thimphu
BANGLADESH
Dhaka
INDIA
BURMA (MYANMAR)
Pyinmana
Rangoon

Hanoi
LAOS
Vientiane
VIETNAM
Bangkok
THAILAND
Phnom Penh
CAMBODIA

Manila
PHILIPPINES

Philippine Sea

South China Sea

Bay of Bengal

Andaman Islands (to India)

Colombo
Nicobar Islands (to India)
Malé
SRI LANKA
MALDIVES

INDIAN OCEAN

Equator

Bandar Seri Begawan
BRUNEI
Kuala Lumpur
Putrajaya
MALAYSIA
SINGAPORE
Singapore
INDONESIA

Dili
EAST TIMOR

New Gu

Jakarta

OCEANIA

AFRICA

China has undergone great political changes in the last century. A painting of Chairman Mao, the late communist leader, hangs over the main gate to the Emperor's old palace in Beijing.

## Key

■ capital city

## Scale 1:56 000 000

0 kms 500    1 000    1 500

# ASIA PHYSICAL

Asia is the world's biggest continent. It is larger than Europe and Africa combined. Rivers flow from the high plateau of Tibet through forests and plains to the surrounding oceans. The heart of Asia is a desert region, including the famous Gobi and Takla Makan. The southern and eastern fringe of Asia is dotted with islands.

## ASIA FACTS

**HIGHEST MOUNTAIN:** Mount Everest 8 850 m

**LONGEST RIVER:** Yangtze 6 380 km

**BIGGEST LAKE:** Caspian Sea 370 999 sq km

**BIGGEST ISLAND:** Borneo 751 100 sq km

**BIGGEST DESERT:** Arabian desert 2 300 000 sq km

**BIGGEST COUNTRY:** Russian Federation 17 075 200 sq km

**SMALLEST COUNTRY:** Maldives 300 sq km

The river Yangtze cuts through deep gorges on its way to the East China Sea. Despite opposition, large dams are being built along the river to generate electricity.

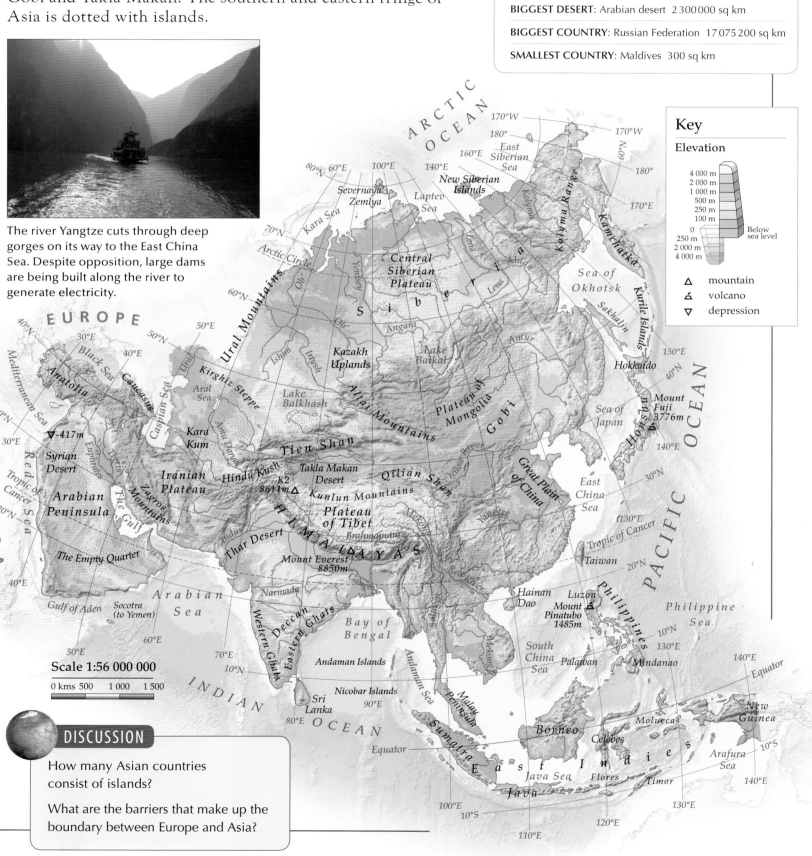

### Key

**Elevation**

4 000 m
2 000 m
1 000 m
500 m
250 m
100 m
0
250 m
2 000 m
4 000 m

Below sea level

△ mountain
◮ volcano
▽ depression

Scale 1:56 000 000

0 kms 500   1 000   1 500

## DISCUSSION

How many Asian countries consist of islands?

What are the barriers that make up the boundary between Europe and Asia?

# ASIA FROM THE SKY

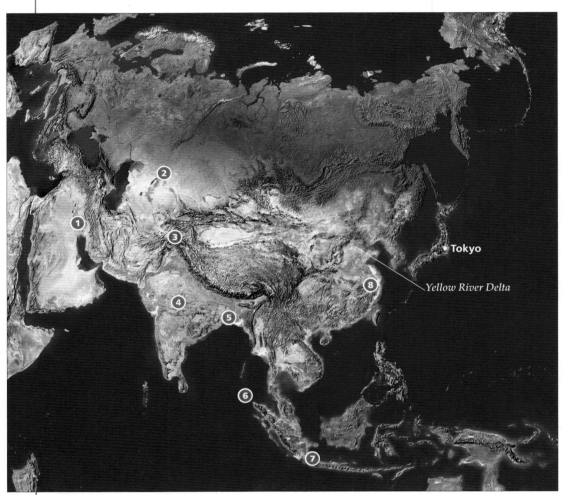

Tokyo

*Yellow River Delta*

## Environmental hotspots

1. Gulf war oil fires, Iraq 1991

2. Water loss, Aral Sea ongoing

3. Earthquake, Pakistan 2005

4. Chemical explosion, Bhopal, India 1984

5. Floods, Bangladesh 1998

6. Tsunami, Banda Aceh, Indonesia 2004

7. Forest fires, Indonesia 1997

8. Polluted cities, China ongoing

The deserts of Saudi Arabia and central Asia are shown in brown on this image. To the north, the green areas depict the forests of Siberia and tundra around the Arctic Ocean.

## Oil fires in the Gulf

February 1991

The smoke from fires set off in the Gulf War polluted the snow in the Himalayas over 3000 km to the east. This photograph shows an oil field set on fires by troops.

## Asia at night

The cities of India, China and Japan show up brightly in this night image. Tibet and western China, mostly being uninhabited, remain in the dark. The lights of Europe appear in the top left-hand corner.

*Honshu*

City boundary, 1860

City boundary, 1964

PACIFIC
OCEAN

2005

## The growth of Tokyo

Tokyo has grown from a population of around 1.5 million in 1860 to 35 million today. The built-up area, shown here in grey blue, has extended across lowland areas to the north and west of the historic core.

## Yellow River delta

The Yellow River in China carries huge quantities of silt down to the sea. This image shows how much the delta has grown in 22 years.

2002

YELLOW SEA

Approximate position
of coastline in 1980

*Yellow River*

## Tsunami damage

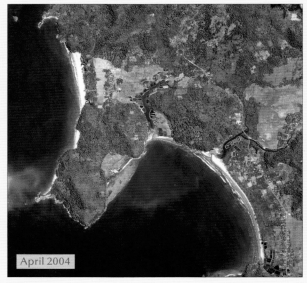

April 2004

This image of northwest Indonesia was taken before the 2004 tsunami. Much of the area is forested, with fields and villages in the lowlands. The beaches show up clearly in white.

January 2005

This image was taken after the tsunami. The brown areas show the deforestation and damage caused by severe flooding. Debris has changed the colour of the sea around the coastline.

# RUSSIAN FEDERATION AND CENTRAL ASIA

The Russian Federation is the world's largest country and is about the same size as Europe and Australia put together. Much of the Russian Federation is covered by coniferous forests, especially Siberia. This vast region is rich in natural resources yet sparsely populated due to the bitterly cold climate. To the south, there are mountains, grasslands and deserts in Kazakhstan and the other central Asian republics.

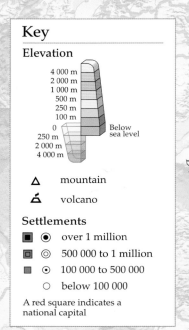

A
B
C
D
93
61
41
5
4
3
2
80°N
30°E
40°E
50°E
70°N
60°N
50°N
40°N
30°N
60°E
70°E
80°E
Franz Josef Land
Barents Sea
Murmansk
Novaya Zemlya
Ostrov Kolguyev
Ostrov Belyy
Poluostrov Yamal
FINLAND
Arctic Circle
White Sea
Baltic Sea
Lake Ladoga
Severodvinsk
Archangel
Saint Petersburg
Kaliningrad
KALININGRAD (to Russ. Fed.)
Pskov
Velikiy Novgorod
Petrozavodsk
Lake Onega
Pechora
Vorkuta
RUSSIA
BELARUS
Smolensk
Tver'
Vologda
Yaroslavl'
Syktyvkar
Moscow
Kineshma
Ural Mountains
Ob'
Ryazan'
Nizhniy Novgorod
Kirov
Glazov
Serov
Surgut
Voronezh
Tambov
Kazan'
Perm'
Izhevsk
UKRAINE
Ul'yanovsk
West Siberian Plain
Yekaterinburg
Ufa
Irtysh
Saratov
Samara
Chelyabinsk
Black Sea
Rostov-na-Donu
Volgograd
Ural'sk
Orenburg
Petropavlovsk
Omsk
Krasnodar
Volga
Ural
Kostanay
Kokshetau
Novosibirsk
Sochi
Stavropol'
Aktobe
Astana
Novokuznetsk
Caucasus
Elbrus 5642m
Astrakhan'
Atyrau
Pavlodar
Nal'chik
Vladikavkaz
Groznyy
KAZAKHSTAN
Karaganda
GEORGIA
Makhachkala
Semipalatinsk
AZERBAIJAN
Aktau
Zhezkazgan
Caspian Sea
Ustyurt Plateau
Aral Sea
Lake Balkhash
Ozero Zaysan
Kzylorda
UZBEKISTAN
Nukus
Daşoguz
Urganch
Syr Darya
Taldykorgan
Bishkek
Almaty
TURKMENISTAN
Tashkent
Pik Khan Tengri 6995m
Aşgabat
Buxoro
Namangan
KYRGYZSTAN
Türkmenabat
Samarqand
Osh
Dushanbe
TAJIKISTAN
IRAN
Mazar-e Sharif
CHINA
Herat
AFGHANISTAN
Asadabad
Kabul
Kandahar
PAKISTAN
N
W
E
S
Key
Elevation
4 000 m
2 000 m
1 000 m
500 m
250 m
100 m
0
250 m
2 000 m
4 000 m
Below sea level
mountain
volcano
Settlements
over 1 million
500 000 to 1 million
100 000 to 500 000
below 100 000
A red square indicates a national capital

Samarqand (Uzbekistan) is located on the historic silk road from China to Europe. This image shows one side of the Registan Square, an architectural wonder that attracts tourists from all over the world.

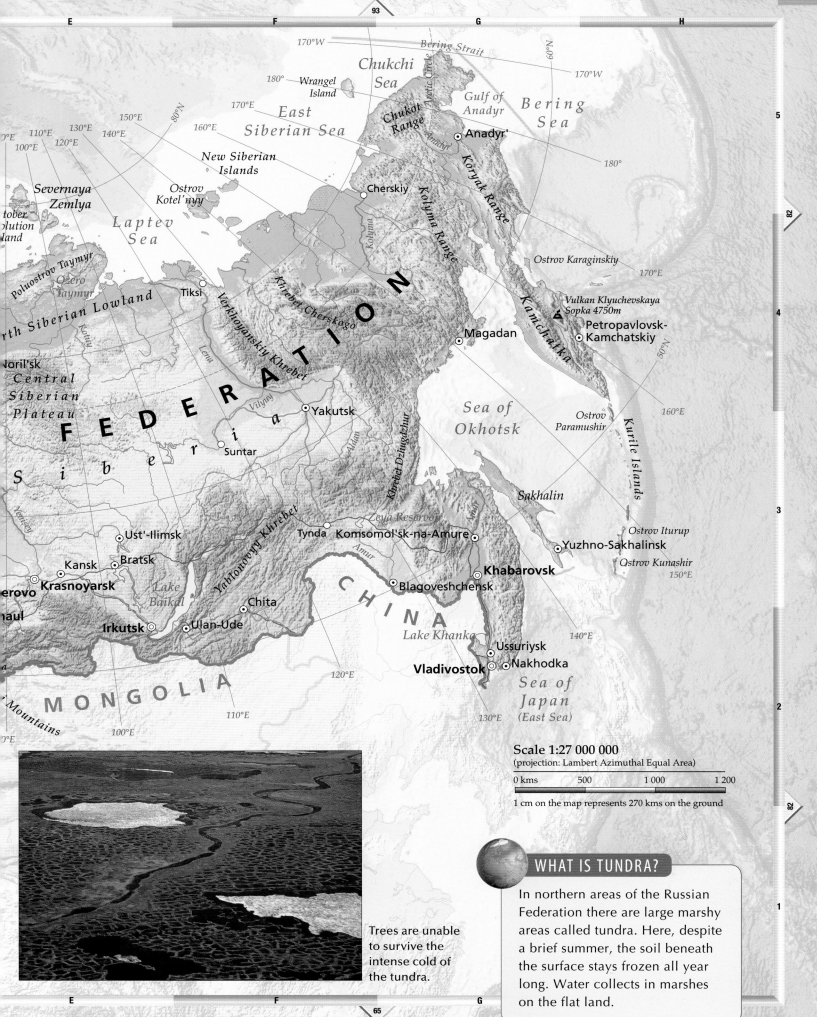

E    F    93    G    H

170°W    Bering Strait    170°W    60°N

*Chukchi Sea*

180°    *Wrangel Island*

170°E    *East Siberian Sea*

*Chukot Range*    *Gulf of Anadyr*    *Bering Sea*

160°E    80°N    ● **Anadyr'**    180°

*New Siberian Islands*    *Koryak Range*

150°E    130°E    140°E

120°E    110°E    100°E

*Severnaya Zemlya*    *Ostrov Kotel'nyy*    ○ Cherskiy    *Kolyma Range*    *Ostrov Karaginskiy*    170°E

tober volution land    *Laptev Sea*    *Khrebet Cherskogo*    *Kamchatka*    *Vulkan Klyuchevskaya Sopka 4750m*

Poluostrov Taymyr    *Kolyma*    *Verkhoyanskiy Khrebet*    **Petropavlovsk- Kamchatskiy**

oril'sk    *Ozero Taymyr*    ○ Tiksi    ● Magadan    50°N

*North Siberian Lowland*    *Lena*    **F E D E R A T I O N**    *Sea of Okhotsk*    *Ostrov Paramushir*    160°E

*Central Siberian Plateau*    *Vilyuy*    ⊙ Yakutsk    *Kurile Islands*

*Kotuy*    *Aldan*

S    i    b    e    r    i    a    ○ Suntar    *Khrebet Dzhugdzhur*    *Sakhalin*    *Ostrov Iturup*

*Nizhniy*    *Zeya Reservoir*    **Khabarovsk**    ● **Yuzhno-Sakhalinsk**    3

Noril'sk    ⊙ Ust'-Ilimsk    Tynda    **Komsomol'sk-na-Amure** ●    *Ostrov Kunashir*    150°E

erovo    Kansk    ● Bratsk    *Yablonovyy Khrebet*    *Amur*    **Khabarovsk**

○ **Krasnoyarsk**    *Lake Baikal*    ● Blagoveshchensk    140°E

aul    Chita    **C H I N A**

**Irkutsk** ⊙    ● Ulan-Ude    *Lake Khanka*    ● Ussuriysk

120°E    ⊙ Nakhodka

**Vladivostok** ●

Mountains    **M O N G O L I A**    110°E    *Sea of Japan (East Sea)*    130°E    140°E    2

100°E

**Scale 1:27 000 000**
(projection: Lambert Azimuthal Equal Area)

0 kms    500    1 000    1 200

1 cm on the map represents 270 kms on the ground

Trees are unable to survive the intense cold of the tundra.

## WHAT IS TUNDRA?

In northern areas of the Russian Federation there are large marshy areas called tundra. Here, despite a brief summer, the soil beneath the surface stays frozen all year long. Water collects in marshes on the flat land.

# WESTERN ASIA AND THE MIDDLE EAST

Turkey and Iran are rugged, mountainous countries. Further south, Syria and Iraq are hotter and drier with deserts that extend to the tip of the Arabian peninsula. The world's largest oil and gas fields are found here. As a result this region plays a crucial part in the world economy.

Like much of the city of Sana, Yemen, the summer palace (Dar al-Hajar) perches on top of rocks.

Baku, on the Caspian Sea, has important oil reserves. However, as the area is landlocked, the oil has to be exported by pipeline. There is widespread pollution around the derricks.

## WHAT IS IRRIGATION?

When it is too dry to grow crops, people sometimes bring water from other places. This is called irrigation. In the past, great civilisations grew up along the banks of rivers like the Tigris and Euphrates, which provided water for irrigation. Today water remains a key resource in the Middle East and the cause of potential conflict.

BULGARIA

*Black Sea*

İstanbul
Zonguldak
Samsun
İzmit
Balıkesir
Bursa
Ankara
Trab
GREECE
*Anatolia*
Sivas
İzmir
Kütahya
TURKE
Aydın
Malatya
Konya
Gazian
Antalya
Adana
Antakya
Alep
Al Ladhiqiyah
SYRI
CYPRUS
Tripoli
Hims
*Mediterranean*
Beirut
*Sea*
LEBANON
Damas
Haifa
*Syr*
Tel Aviv-Yafo
Irbid
*Des*
Jerusalem
Amman
Be'er Sheva'
*Dead Sea*
ISRAEL  JORDAN
*Gulf of Suez*
Jabal al Lawz
△ 2580m
Tabūk
Ḍubā
E G Y P T
Medina
*Tropic of Cancer*
*Red Sea*
Jedda
SUDAN
Mec
ERITREA

30°E
35°E
40°N
35°N
30°E
30°N
35°E
25°N
20°N

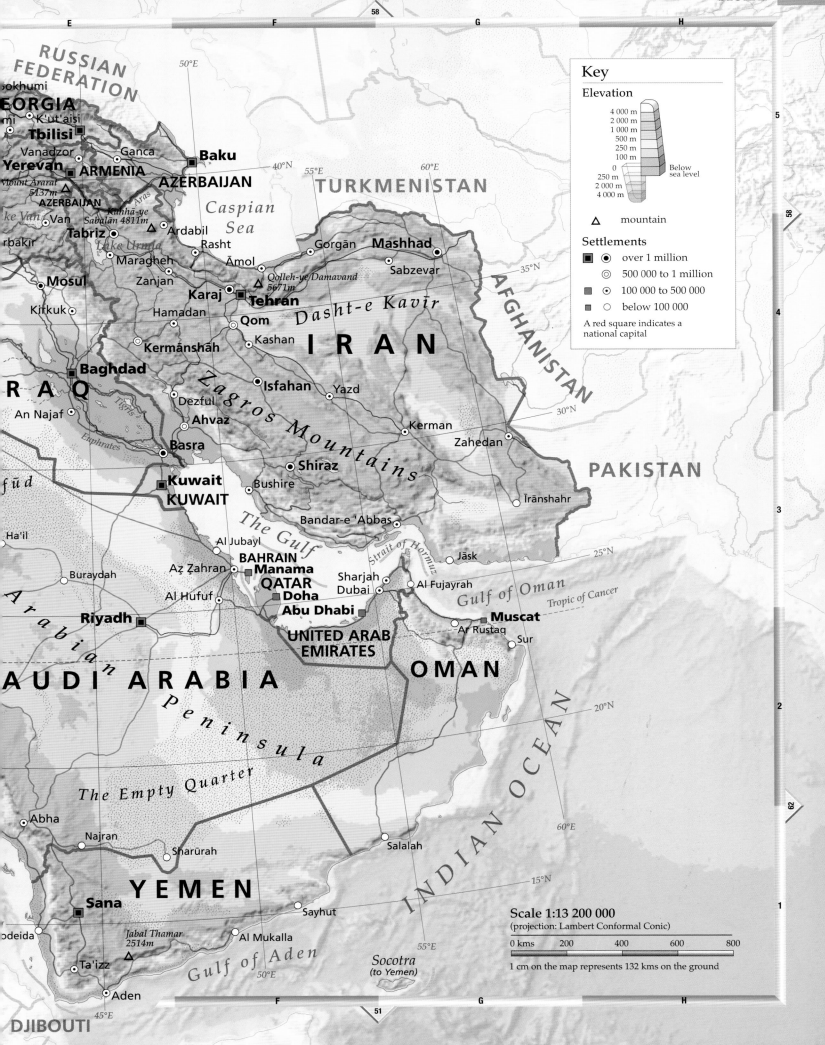

RUSSIAN FEDERATION

GEORGIA
okhumi
mi K'ut'aisi
**Tbilisi**
Vanadzor Ganca
**Yerevan** ARMENIA **Baku**
AZERBAIJAN
AZERBAIJAN
Mount Ararat
5137m
ke Van Van
rbakir **Tabriz** Ardabil
Lake Urmia Rasht
Maragheh Āmol
**Mosul** Zanjan
Kirkuk **Karaj** Tehran
Hamadan
An Najaf Qom
**Kermanshah** Kashan
**Baghdad**
IRAQ Dezful
**Isfahan** Yazd
**Ahvaz**
Euphrates
**Basra**
Tigris
**Kuwait**
KUWAIT Bushire
Ha'il
Al Jubayl
Buraydah
Az Zahran **BAHRAIN**
Al Hufuf **Manama**
QATAR
**Doha**
**Riyadh** **Abu Dhabi**
UNITED ARAB
EMIRATES

Caspian
Sea
Aras
Kuhhā-ye
Sabalān 4811m
Gorgān **Mashhad**
Sabzevar
Qolleh-ye Damavand
5671m
Dasht-e Kavir
IRAN
Kerman
Zahedan
Īrānshahr
Bandar-e 'Abbas
The Gulf
Strait of Hormuz
Jāsk
Gulf of Oman
Sharjah
Dubai Al Fujayrah
**Muscat**
Ar Rustaq
Sur

TURKMENISTAN

AFGHANISTAN

PAKISTAN

OMAN

fūd
Arabian
AUDI ARABIA
Peninsula
The Empty Quarter
Abha
Najran
Sharūrah
YEMEN
**Sana**
Jabal Thamar
2514m
odeida
Ta'izz
Al Mukalla
Salalah
Sayhut
Gulf of Aden
Socotra
(to Yemen)
Aden

Tropic of Cancer

INDIAN OCEAN

DJIBOUTI

Scale 1:13 200 000
(projection: Lambert Conformal Conic)

0 kms 200 400 600 800

1 cm on the map represents 132 kms on the ground

# SOUTH ASIA

South Asia is bounded by the Himalayas to the north, and seas and oceans in other directions. Three great rivers, the Indus, Ganges and Brahmaputra, provide water from the mountains for farming on the plains. Nearly a quarter of the world's population lives in this region. Although there are many large cities, most people still live in traditional villages.

Busy street markets, where people sell produce from surrounding areas, are a common sight in Indian towns.

## Key

### Elevation

4 000 m
2 000 m
1 000 m
500 m
250 m
100 m
0
250 m
2 000 m
4 000 m

Below sea level

△ mountain

### Settlements

■ ⊙ over 1 million
▣ ◎ 500 000 to 1 million
▪ ⊙ 100 000 to 500 000
▪ ○ below 100 000

A red square indicates a national capital

Buses and lorries are common forms of transport on long-distance roads. There are relatively few private cars, but train travel is cheap and India has a vast railway network.

AFGHANISTAN

Hindu Ku

35°N
70°E

Khyber Pass 1080m

Ming

Muzaffara

**Peshawar**

**Islamabad**

**Rawalpindi**

Gujra

**Gujranwal**

**Laho**

**Faisalabad**

65°E

Toba Kakar Range

Sulaiman Range

Chenab

30°N

◎ **Quetta**

Nushki ○

Central Makran Range

○ **Multan**

Sutlej

Bahawalp

**PAKISTAN**

Rahimyar Khan

Shikarpur ⊙

IRAN

Dasht

Nāl

Indus

Thar Desert

Bik

25°N

○ Gwadar

○ Turbat

Nawabshah ⊙

**Jodhpur** ◎

Ajr

**Hyderabad**

Mirpur Khas ⊙

**Karachi** ■

Sujawal ⊙

Tropic of Cancer

Mouths of the Indus

65°E

Rann of Kachchh

Gandhidham ⊙

**Ahmadabad** ■

Gulf of Kachchh

Jamnagar ⊙

◎ **Rajkot**

**Vadodara**

Porbandar ○

Kathiawar Peninsula

**Surat**

N

**Nashik**

W — E

20°N

Gulf of Khambhat

S

**Kalyan**

**Mumbai** ■
(Bombay)

Pu

70°E

Arabian Sea

West e

Kolhapur ⊙

Belgaum

Panaji ⊙

15°N

Hub

Mangalore

Amindivi Islands

70°E

Cannano

Laccadive Islands (Lakshadweep)

Ca

○ Kavaratti

10°N

Minicoy Island

70°E

**MALDIVES**

Maldive Islands

5°N

75°

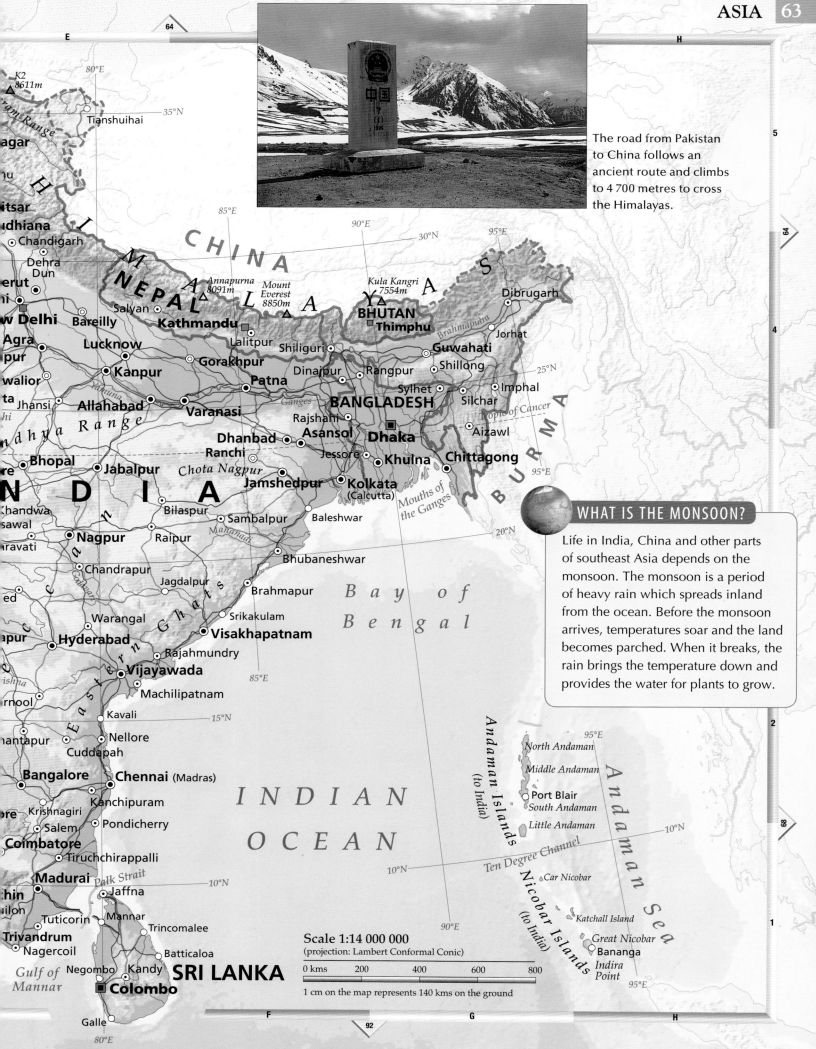

The road from Pakistan to China follows an ancient route and climbs to 4 700 metres to cross the Himalayas.

## WHAT IS THE MONSOON?

Life in India, China and other parts of southeast Asia depends on the monsoon. The monsoon is a period of heavy rain which spreads inland from the ocean. Before the monsoon arrives, temperatures soar and the land becomes parched. When it breaks, the rain brings the temperature down and provides the water for plants to grow.

K2
8611m
Tianshuihai
35°N
80°E

aram Range
agar
nu
udhiana
Chandigarh
Dehra Dun
erut
ni
w Delhi
Bareilly
Agra
pur
walior
ta
Jhansi
hi
Allahabad
dhya Range
NDIA
Bhopal
Khandwa
sawal
Nagpur
aravati
Chandrapur
ed
apur
Hyderabad
Bangalore
re
Krishnagiri
Salem
Coimbatore
Tiruchchirappalli
Madurai
hin
uilon
Trivandrum
Nagercoil
Tuticorin

CHINA

NEPAL
Salyan
Lucknow
Kanpur
Patna
Varanasi
Ganges
Kathmandu
Lalitpur
Gorakhpur
Dinajpur
Dhanbad
Asansol
Ranchi
Jessore
Jamshedpur
Kolkata
(Calcutta)
Chota Nagpur
Bilaspur
Sambalpur
Baleshwar
Raipur
Jagdalpur
Brahmapur
Bhubaneshwar
Warangal
Srikakulam
Visakhapatnam
Rajahmundry
Vijayawada
Machilipatnam
Kavali
Nellore
Cuddapah
Chennai (Madras)
Kanchipuram
Pondicherry
Jaffna

HIMALAYAS
Annapurna 8091m
Mount Everest 8850m
Kula Kangri 7554m
BHUTAN
Thimphu
Brahmaputra
Shiliguri
Rangpur
Guwahati
Shillong
BANGLADESH
Rajshahi
Dhaka
Khulna
Chittagong
Sylhet
Silchar
Tropic of Cancer
Aizawl
Dibrugarh
Jorhat
Imphal

BURMA

Bay of Bengal

Mouths of the Ganges

Mahanadi

Eastern Ghats

INDIAN OCEAN

Andaman Islands (to India)
North Andaman
Middle Andaman
Port Blair
South Andaman
Little Andaman

Andaman Sea

Nicobar Islands (to India)
Car Nicobar
Ten Degree Channel
Katchall Island
Great Nicobar
Bananga
Indira Point

Palk Strait
Mannar
Trincomalee
Batticaloa
Gulf of Mannar
Negombo
Kandy
SRI LANKA
Colombo
Galle

30°N
85°E
90°E
95°E
25°N
20°N
95°E
95°E
15°N
10°N
10°N
85°E
90°E
95°E
80°E
10°N

**Scale 1:14 000 000**
(projection: Lambert Conformal Conic)

0 kms   200   400   600   800

1 cm on the map represents 140 kms on the ground

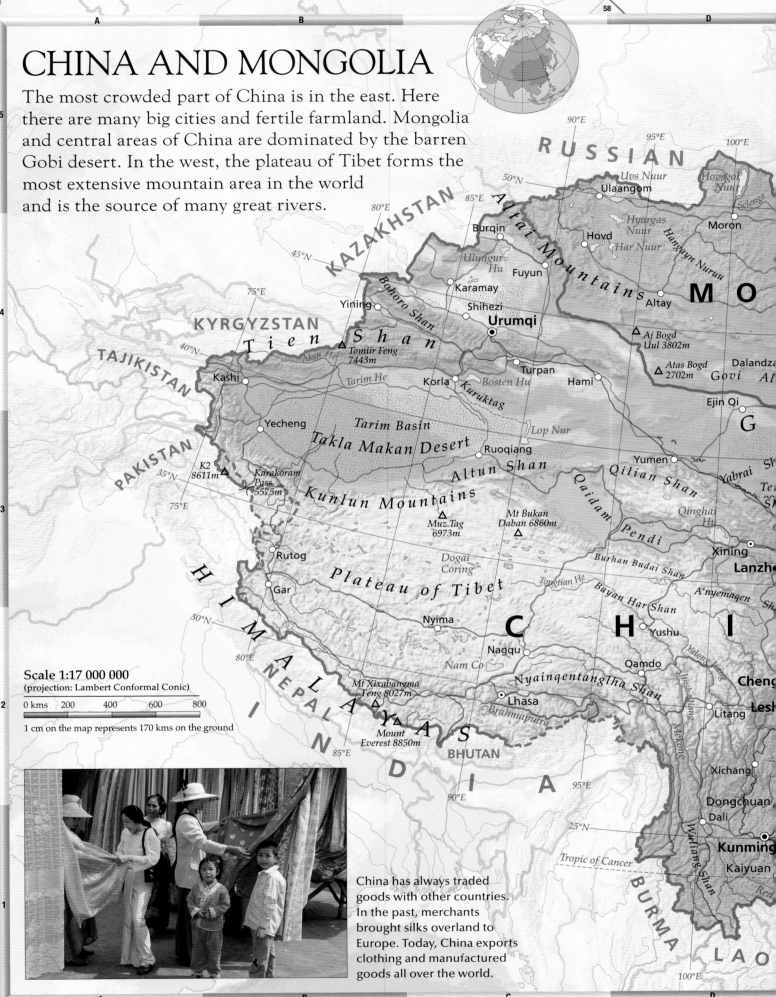

# CHINA AND MONGOLIA

The most crowded part of China is in the east. Here there are many big cities and fertile farmland. Mongolia and central areas of China are dominated by the barren Gobi desert. In the west, the plateau of Tibet forms the most extensive mountain area in the world and is the source of many great rivers.

58

RUSSIAN

KAZAKHSTAN

KYRGYZSTAN

TAJIKISTAN

PAKISTAN

Uvs Nuur
Ulaangom
Hovsgol Nuur
Hyargas Nuur
Moron
Burqin
Hovd
Har Nuur
Selenga
Hangayn Nuruu
MO
Yining
Karamay
Fuyun
Altay
Aj Bogd Uul 3802m
Shihezi
Urumqi
Atas Bogd 2702m
Dalandza
Tien Shan
Tomiir Feng 7443m
Aksu He
Turpan
Hami
Govi Al
Kashi
Bosten Hu
Korla
Kuruktag
Tarim He
Ejin Qi
G
Yecheng
Tarim Basin
Lop Nur
Yumen
Takla Makan Desert
Ruoqiang
Qilian Shan
Yabrai
K2 8611m
Altun Shan
Te
S
Karakoram Pass 5575m
Qaidam Pendi
Xining
Kunlun Mountains
Qinghai Hu
Lanzh
Muz Tag 6973m
Mt Bukan Daban 6860m
Rutog
Burhan Budai Shan
Dogai Coring
A'nyemaqen
Sh
Gar
Plateau of Tibet
Tongtian He
Bayan Har Shan
Yushu
C
H
I
HIMALAYA
Nyima
Nagqu
Qamdo
Cheng
Nam Co
Nyainqentanglha Shan
Litang
Lesh
Mt Xixabangma Feng 8027m
Lhasa
Brahmaputra
NEPAL
Mount Everest 8850m
BHUTAN
Xichang
INDIA
Dongchuan
Dali
BURMA
Tropic of Cancer
Kunming
Kaiyuan
LAO

50°N
45°N
40°N
35°N
30°N
25°N
80°E
85°E
90°E
95°E
100°E
75°E
90°E
95°E
100°E

## Scale 1:17 000 000
(projection: Lambert Conformal Conic)

0 kms   200   400   600   800

1 cm on the map represents 170 kms on the ground

China has always traded goods with other countries. In the past, merchants brought silks overland to Europe. Today, China exports clothing and manufactured goods all over the world.

N

E

S

EDERATION

OLIA

**ühbaatar**

**an Bator**

**Darhan**

Qin Gol

Kerulen

**Ondorhaan**

**Manzhouli**

**Choybalsan**

Hulun Nur

Menengiyn Tal

Amur

Mohe

**Jagdaqi**

Argun

Nen jiang

Great Khingan Range

Xiao Hinggan Ling

**Zalantun**

**Qiqihar**

**Jiamusi**

Ussuri

**Jixi**

**Harbin**

**Mudanjiang**

Lake Khanka

**Baicheng**

**Jilin**

**Yanji**

**Xilinhot**

**Erenhot**

**Tongliao**

Manchuria

**Changchun**

**Shenyang**

**Chifeng**

**Fuxin**

**Chengde**

**Anshan**

**NORTH KOREA**

**Hohhot**

**Beijing**

**Dandong**

Korea Bay

**SOUTH KOREA**

**Baotou**

**Datong**

**Tangshan**

**Tianjin**

**Dalian**

**Yinchuan**

Yellow River

Great Wall of China

**Shijiazhuang**

Bo Hai

**Yantai**

Yellow Sea

**Taiyuan**

**Weifang**

**Handan**

**Jinan**

**Qingdao**

**Zhengzhou**

**Jining**

**Linyi**

ongchuan

**Luoyang**

**Xuzhou**

**Yancheng**

**Xi'an**

Hongze Hu

A

Han Shui

**Nanjing**

East China Sea

nuan ndi

**Hefei**

Tai Hu

**Shanghai**

anxian

**Wuhan**

**Hangzhou**

Yangtze

**Yichang**

**Ningbo**

Dongting Hu

Poyang Hu

**Jinhua**

**Chongqing**

**Nanchang**

**Jingdezhen**

**Wenzhou**

**Changsha**

**Pingxiang**

**Fuzhou**

nyi

**Huaihua**

**Hengyang**

**Fuzhou**

anshui

**Ganzhou**

**Yong'an**

**Taipei**

**Guiyang**

**Yongzhou**

**T'aichung**

Tropic of Cancer

nshun

**Guilin**

**Shaoguan**

**Longyan**

Taiwan

**Liuzhou**

**Hezhou**

**Xiamen**

**T'ainan**

Taiwan Strait

se

**Zhaoqing**

**Guangzhou**

**Shantou**

**TAIWAN**

anning

**Dongguan**

**Kaohsiung**

**Yulin**

**Hong Kong**

**Beihai**

**Maoming**

South China Sea

Luzon Strait

**Zhanjiang**

Gulf of Tongking

**Haikou**

Hainan Dao

**PHILIPPINES**

There are 34 cities in China with a population of over 1 million people. Shanghai is the largest city with 17 million inhabitants. As cities grow larger, air and water pollution have become a serious problem.

## WHY DO DESERTS SPREAD?

The land on the edge of a desert usually receives very little rain. If people cut down trees or overuse the land, the desert may spread. Desertification is a serious threat in many parts of the world. In China, dust from the Gobi desert often blows as far as the capital city, Beijing.

# KOREA AND JAPAN

Japan consists of four main islands and over 3000 smaller ones. More than three-quarters of the land is taken up by high, volcanic mountains so most people live crowded together on the coastal plains. Japan is a major industrial nation with global car and electronics industries. On the mainland, South Korea has also developed high-tech and manufacturing industries. North Korea, which has a communist government, remains isolated from the rest of the world.

### Key

**Elevation**

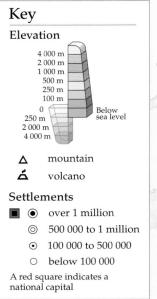

4 000 m
2 000 m
1 000 m
500 m
250 m
100 m
0
250 m
2 000 m
4 000 m

Below sea level

△    mountain

▲    volcano

**Settlements**

■ ⊙    over 1 million

◎    500 000 to 1 million

⊙    100 000 to 500 000

○    below 100 000

A red square indicates a national capital

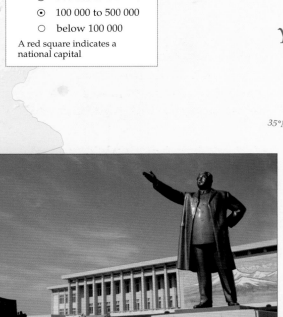

This great square in the centre of Pyongyang is used for parades and celebrations.

RUSSIAN FEDERATION

CHINA

Hoeryŏng

Paektu-san 2750m ▲

Najin

Huch'ang

Hyesan

Ch'ŏngjin

125°E

Kanggye

Kimch'aek

Sinuiju

Yalu

Huich'ŏn

40°N

Chongju

Sinp'o

Hamhung

40°N

Sinmi-do

Korea Bay

Pyŏngyang

Namp'o

Sariwon

Wonsan

**NORTH KOREA**

Kosong

East Korea Bay

Haeju

(Ceasefire line since 1953)

Ongjin

Kaesong

Ch'unch'on

Sokch'o

Kangnung

Inch'on

**Seoul**

Suwon

Tonghae

Liancourt Rocks (disputed)

Ch'onan

Wonju

Ch'ungju

**SOUTH KOREA**

*Yellow Sea*

**Taejon**

Andong

Oki-shoto

Dozen

Kunsan

Chŏnju

**Taegu**

P'ohang

35°N

**Ulsan**

**Kwangju**

Chinju

**Pusan**

Matsue

Mokp'o

Sunch'on

Koje-do

Korea Strait

Chugoku-san

125°E

Chin-do

Kogum-do

Namhae-do

Tsushima

Masuda

**Okayam**

Ko-saki

Yamaguchi

**Hiroshima**

Cheju-do

Goto-retto

**Kitakyushu**

Matsuyama

Iyo-nada

*Shiko*

**Fukuoka**

Sasebo

Kurume

Oita

Uwajima

Nagasaki

**Kumamoto**

Nakamura

Amakusa-nada

Yatsushiro

Nobeoka

Koshikijima-retto

Sendai

*Kyushu*

Miyazaki

*East China Sea*

**Kagoshima**

Miyakonojō

Shibushi-wan

Tanega-shima

Yaku-shima

30°N

30°N

130°E

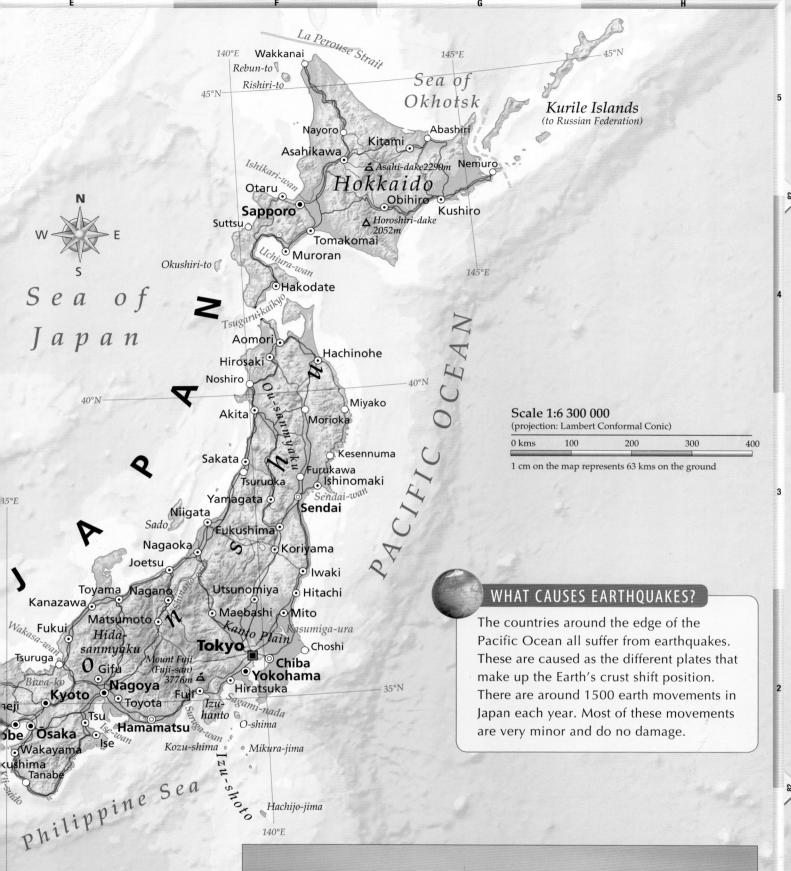

E F 59 G H

140°E Wakkanai

La Perouse Strait

*Rebun-to* 45°N

*Rishiri-to*

Sea of
Okhotsk

Kurile Islands
*(to Russian Federation)*

45°N

Nayoro Abashiri

Asahikawa Kitami

*Ishikari-wan* Nemuro

△ *Asahi-dake* 2290m

Otaru *Hokkaido*

**Sapporo** Obihiro Kushiro

Suttsu

△ *Horoshiri-dake*
2052m

Tomakomai

Muroran

*Okushiri-to* *Uchiura-wan*

Hakodate

Sea of
Japan

*Tsugaru-kaikyo*

Aomori

Hirosaki Hachinohe

Noshiro 40°N

40°N Akita Miyako

Morioka

Sakata

Tsuruoka Ishinomaki

Yamagata Furukawa

Niigata *Sendai-wan*

*Sado* **Sendai**

Fukushima

Nagaoka Koriyama

Joetsu Iwaki

Toyama Utsunomiya Hitachi

Kanazawa Nagano Maebashi Mito

Fukui Matsumoto *Kasumiga-ura*

*Hida-
sanmyaku* **Tokyo** Choshi

Tsuruga *Kanto Plain*

Gifu **Chiba**

*Biwa-ko* Mount Fuji **Yokohama**
(*Fuji-san*)

**Kyoto** **Nagoya** 3776m △ Hiratsuka

Tsu Toyota Fuji

**Ōsaka** **Hamamatsu** *Izu-
hanto*

Wakayama Ise *Sagami-nada* 35°N

*O-shima*

Tanabe

*Kozu-shima* *Izu-shoto*

*Mikura-jima*

Philippine Sea

*Hachijo-jima*

140°E

PACIFIC OCEAN

**Scale 1:6 300 000**
(projection: Lambert Conformal Conic)

| 0 kms | 100 | 200 | 300 | 400 |

1 cm on the map represents 63 kms on the ground

## WHAT CAUSES EARTHQUAKES?

The countries around the edge of the
Pacific Ocean all suffer from earthquakes.
These are caused as the different plates that
make up the Earth's crust shift position.
There are around 1500 earth movements in
Japan each year. Most of these movements
are very minor and do no damage.

Tokyo has developed
from a sixteenth century
castle town to become
one of the largest cities
in the world.

# SOUTHEAST ASIA

Rainforests once covered the lowland areas of southeast Asia. Many of these forests have now been cleared to create space for farming, factories and houses. Indonesia is the biggest and most populous country in the region. It is over 5000 km across and made up of more than 13000 islands. The Philippines is another island nation with modern industries.

## Key

### Elevation

4 000 m
2 000 m
1 000 m
500 m
250 m
100 m
0
250 m
2 000 m
4 000 m

Below sea level

### Settlements

| | |
|---|---|
| ■ ⊙ | over 1 million |
| ◎ | 500 000 to 1 million |
| ■ ⊙ | 100 000 to 500 000 |
| ■ ○ | below 100 000 |

A red square indicates a national capital

△ mountain     ⚊ volcano

N
W   E
S

Singapore, the smallest country in Asia, has developed from a port into a major industrial city.

Scale 1:18 200 000
(projection: Mercator)

| 0 kms | 250 | 500 | 750 | 1 000 |

1 cm on the map represents 182 kms on the ground

As well as creating a unique habitat, the dense vegetation of the rainforest protects the soil from erosion in heavy rain.

Buddhism is widespread in southeast Asia. The temples attract visitors from all over the world.

## WHAT IS AN ARCHIPELAGO?

An archipelago is a group or chain of islands. Some archipelagos are the tops of flooded mountain ranges. Others, such as the Philippines, have been raised up from the ocean floor due to Earth movements or volcanic activity.

### Map labels

66

G H

5

84

*South China Sea*

120°E
20°N Luzon Strait 20°N
*Babuyan Channel*
125°E
*Luzon*
Cordillera Central
Ilagan
Dagupan
15°N Mount Pinatubo 15°N
1485m △
**Manila** ■ Cabanatuan
Lucena
Calapan Naga
*Mindoro* Legaspi
*Sibuyan Sea* Calbayog
Roxas City *Samar*
**PHILIPPINES** Cadiz Tacloban
10°N 10°N Cebu
115°E *Panay Island* *Leyte*
*Negros*
Puerto Princesa *Bohol Sea* Butuan
*Palawan Passage* Iligan
*Palawan* Bislig
*Sulu Sea*
Balabac Strait **Davao**
Gunung *Moro Gulf* *Mindanao*
Kinabalu 4101m △ Zamboanga
Sandakan *Basilan* *Davao Gulf*
**Bandar Seri Begawan** General Santos
**BRUNEI**
Sabah *Sulu Archipelago* 5°N
Miri Tawau *Kepulauan Talaud*
*Borneo* *Celebes Sea*

*Xiracel Islands (disputed)*

*Spratly Islands (disputed)*

**PALAU**

G
H
4
2
74
5°S
10°S

*Pacel Islands (disputed)*

*PACIFIC OCEAN*

*Philippine Sea*

*awak* Sarawak
*man*
*Pegunungan Muller*
*Kalimantan*
Samarinda
Balikpapan
*jit*
*njarmasin*

*Pulau Morotai*
*Pulau Halmahera*
Manado
Gorontalo Mafa *Molucca Sea*
Gulf of Tomini Waigeo
*Halmahera Sea*
Palu Sorong Doberai Peninsula
*Kepulauan Banggai* Misool
*Celebes* *Kepulauan Sula* *Ceram Sea* Fakfak
Parepare Waflia *Ceram*
Kendari *Pulau Buru* Ambon
*Moluccas*
**INDONESIA**
**Ujungpandang** *Pulau Buton*
*va Sea* *Banda Sea* *Kepulauan Kai*
*narang* *Flores Sea*
**Surabaya** *Pulau Wetar* *Pulau Yamdena*
Jember *Lesser Sunda Islands* Pulau Wetar
*Pulau Lombok* Sumbawa *Kepulauan Alor*
*Bali* Flores *Kepulauan Leti*
**Malang** Mataram *Kepulauan Tanimbar*
*Kediri* Denpasar Endeh **Dili**
*Madiun* Waikabubak **EAST TIMOR**
*rakarta* *Selat Sumba* *Savu Sea* *Timor*
*Pulau Sumba* Kupang
115°E 120°E 125°E 130°E

*Makassar Strait*
*Pegunungan Quarles*

*Teluk Cenderawasih*
*Pulau Biak*
Sarmi
Jayapura
*Sungai Mamberamo*
*Pegunungan Maoke*
Puncak Jaya 5040m △
Amamapare
*New Guinea*
Papua (Irian Jaya)
**PAPUA NEW GUINEA**

Equator
135°E 140°E
5°S
*Arafura Sea*
10°S 10°S
Torres Strait
135°E 140°E

E F G H
74

# OCEANIA POLITICAL

Australia is by far the largest and most populous country in Oceania. Like New Zealand, it was once a British colony but it has been independent for over 100 years. To the north, Papua New Guinea is another significant country. To the east, there are numerous island states dotted across the Pacific Ocean.

## Key

■ capital city
□ dependency capital city

Scale 1:56 000 000

0 kms  600  1 200  1 800  2 400

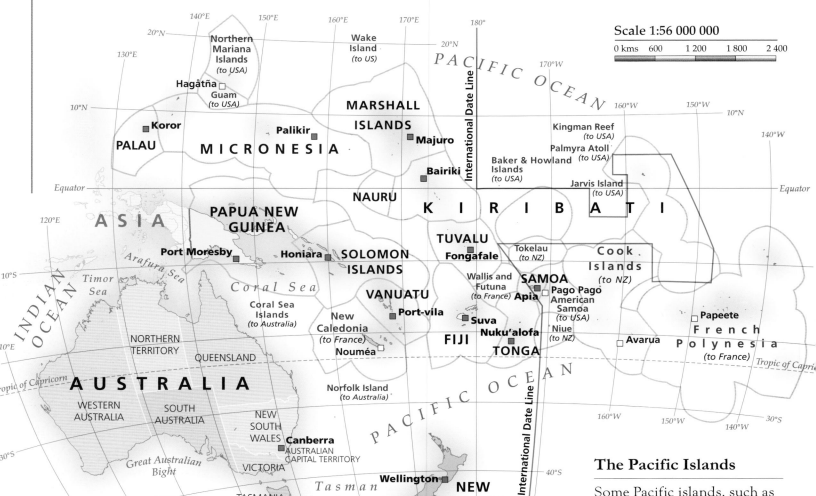

## The Pacific Islands

Some Pacific islands, such as New Caledonia and Guam, still belong to other countries. Others are tiny, independent nations. The Polynesians, who were the original people to settle in these remote areas, remain the main population group today.

The island nation of Nauru is so small that it does not have a capital. Nauru has long been dependent on phosphate exported to Australia for national income. Now that the mineral is almost exhausted, Nauruans must find another way of securing their financial future.

# OCEANIA PHYSICAL

Oceania is the smallest continent. It is made of up Australia, New Zealand, Papua New Guinea and over 20 000 small Pacific islands. Most of Oceania lies within the Tropics. Although surrounded by water, Australia is famous for its deserts. New Zealand and New Guinea have mountainous landscapes. Many of the small islands are ancient volcanoes that have sunk back into the sea and are now only a few metres above sea level.

## OCEANIA FACTS

**HIGHEST MOUNTAIN:** Mount Wilhelm  4 509 m

**LONGEST RIVER:** Murray/Darling  3 718 km

**BIGGEST LAKE:** Lake Eyre  9 000 km

**BIGGEST ISLAND:** New Guinea  800 000 sq km

**BIGGEST DESERT:** Great Victoria Desert  424 400 sq km

**BIGGEST COUNTRY:** Australia  7 686 850 sq km

**SMALLEST COUNTRY:** Nauru  21 sq km

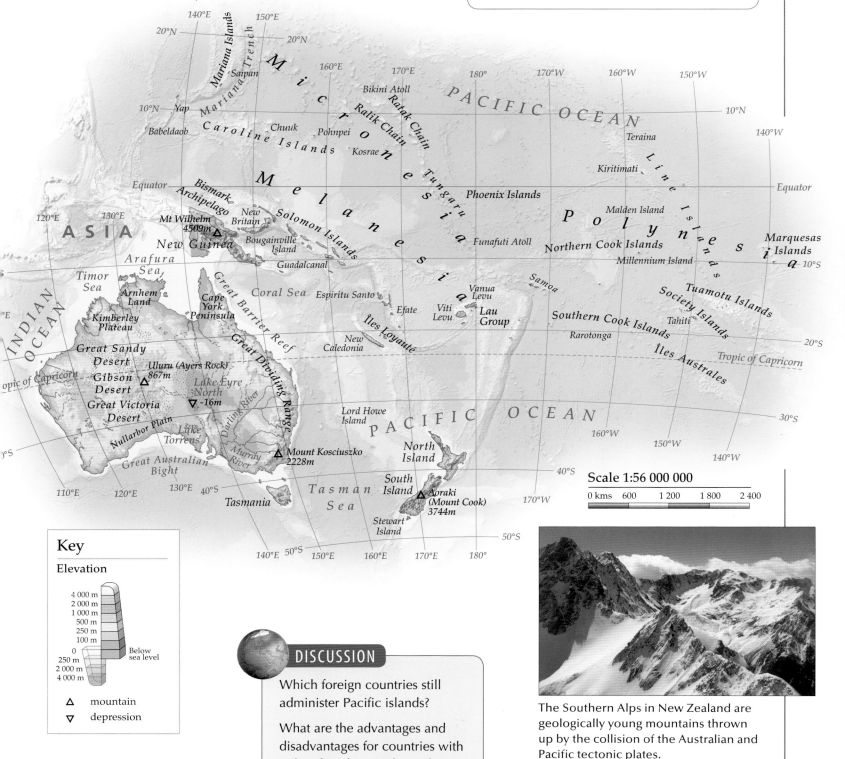

## Key

### Elevation

4 000 m
2 000 m
1 000 m
500 m
250 m
100 m
0
250 m
2 000 m
4 000 m
Below sea level

△  mountain
▽  depression

Scale 1:56 000 000

0 kms  600  1 200  1 800  2 400

### DISCUSSION

Which foreign countries still administer Pacific islands?

What are the advantages and disadvantages for countries with only a few thousand people?

The Southern Alps in New Zealand are geologically young mountains thrown up by the collision of the Australian and Pacific tectonic plates.

# OCEANIA FROM THE SKY

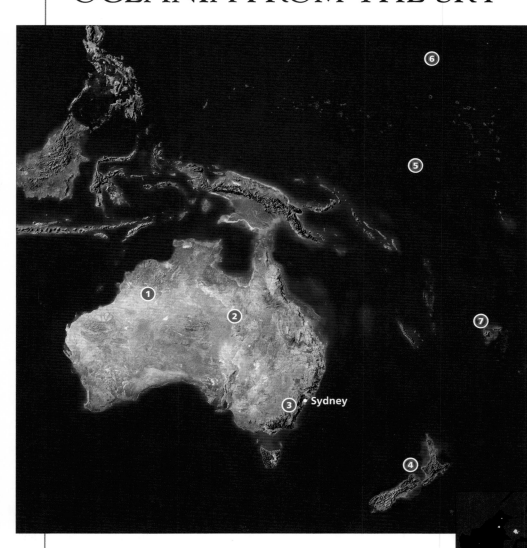

## Environmental hotspots

1. **Desertification, Australia ongoing**

2. **Air pollution, Mount Isa mine, Australia ongoing**

3. **Bush fires, New South Wales, Australia 2001, 2002, 2004**

4. **Ozone hole, New Zealand 1980s onwards**

5. **Soil contamination and vegetation loss, Phosphate mines, Nauru 1908 onwards**

6. **Nuclear test site, Bikini Atoll, Marshall Islands 1940s and 1950s**

7. **Degraded coral reefs, Fiji ongoing**

The deserts and shallow coastal areas around Australia are a striking feature in this satellite image. The mountains and forests of New Guinea are clearly shown to the north.

## Oceania at night

Apart from Antarctica, Oceania is the least populous continent. The night image shows great empty areas in Australia and New Guinea. The main settlements are all on the coastline.

## Nuclear tests

26th March 1954

The United States, France and Britain have all conducted nuclear testing in the remote Pacific Islands. The most famous site, Bikini Atoll, was used in the 1940s and 1950s and still suffers high levels of background radiation.

## Sydney harbour

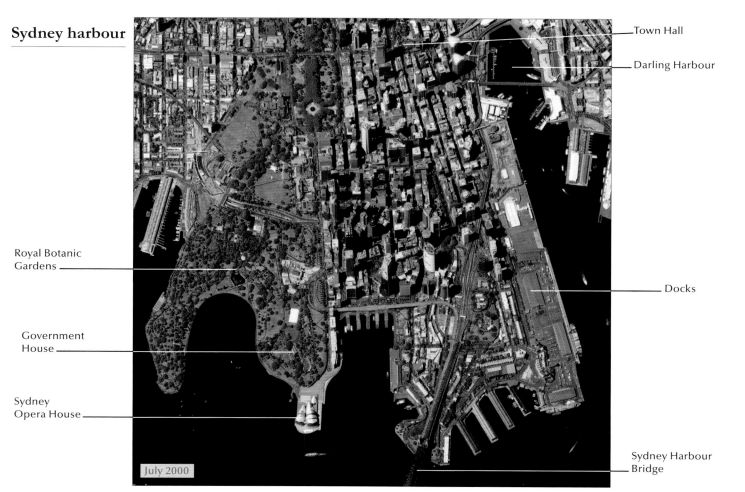

Town Hall

Darling Harbour

Royal Botanic Gardens

Government House

Sydney Opera House

Docks

Sydney Harbour Bridge

July 2000

This aerial view shows the central business district of Sydney. It has developed around the first European settlement, which was founded in 1778.

## Coral island, Kiribati

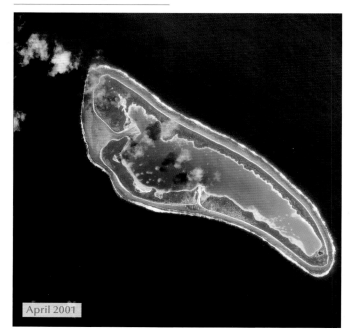

April 2001

Coral islands are scattered across the Pacific Ocean. The colour of the water shows the difference between the shallow lagoon and deep surrounding ocean. Being a few metres high, coral islands are vulnerable to rising sea levels.

## Bush fires

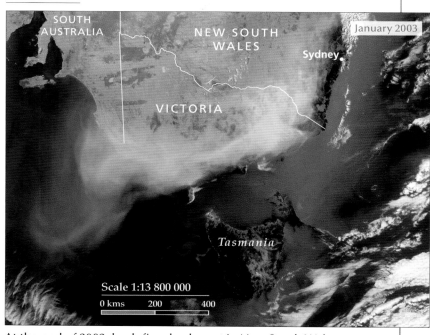

SOUTH AUSTRALIA

NEW SOUTH WALES

January 2003

Sydney

VICTORIA

Tasmania

Scale 1:13 800 000

0 kms    200    400

At the end of 2002, bush fires broke out in New South Wales, Australia after a prolonged period of drought. At one time, there were as many as 85 fires with flames up to 30 metres high, fanned by strong winds.

# AUSTRALIA AND NEW ZEALAND

Australia is the sixth largest country in the world. Deserts and scrubland cover much of the centre (or outback) of the island. Along the eastern coast, the Great Dividing Range forms the most mountainous area of Australia. The majority of Australians have settled in this area. 2000 kilometres further east, New Zealand is one of the world's most isolated countries. It is divided into two main islands. The North Island is volcanic and the South Island is dominated by the Southern Alps.

Sydney Opera House is one of the world's most famous buildings. With a roof like a ship's sails, it has come to represent Australia.

This atoll is one of many threatened by rising sea levels in Tuvalu (see pages 70–71). The coral, which has been growing for up to 30 million years, will die if there are sudden climate changes.

EAST TIMOR

*Arafura Sea*

*Timor Sea*

Darwin

*Arnhem Land*

Katherine

Wyndham

*Kimberley Plateau*

NORTHERN TERRITORY

Broome

Halls Creek

*Tanami Desert*

Tennant Cr

*Great Sandy Desert*

Lake Mackay

*Macdonnell Ranges*

Alice Sprin

Dampier

*Hamersley Range*

Newman

A U S T R

Exmouth

Tropic of Capricorn

△ Uluru (Ayers Rock) 867m

*Musgrave Ranges*

Sim De

Carnarvon

WESTERN AUSTRALIA

SOUTH AUSTRA

Lake Ey Nor

Mount Magnet

*Great Victoria Desert*

Coob

Geraldton

Reid

Kalgoorlie

*Nullarbor Plain*

Eucla

Ceduna

*Great Australian Bight*

P Augu

Peterb

Merredin

Perth

Fremantle

Esperance

Port Lincoln

Ade

Augusta

Albany

## WHAT IS AN ATOLL?

Dense colonies of coral grow in the shallow waters around the islands of the South Pacific. Over time the coral builds up into reefs, creating lagoons around the coast. Sometimes the land sinks back into the sea, due to erosion or changes in the seabed, and the lagoon is left behind. This is known as an atoll.

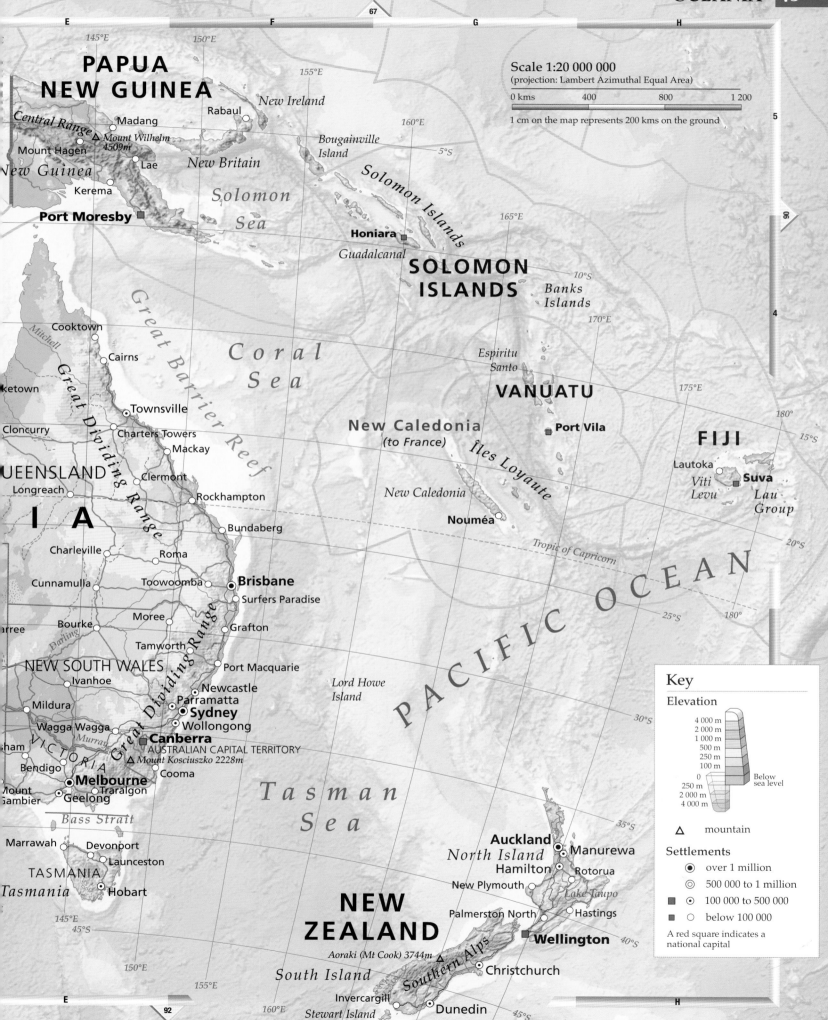

**PAPUA NEW GUINEA**

*Central Range* · Madang · Rabaul · *New Ireland*

145°E  150°E  155°E

Mount Hagen · △ Mount Wilhelm 4509m

Lae

*New Guinea*

Kerema

*New Britain*

■ **Port Moresby**

*Solomon Sea*

160°E

*Bougainville Island*

5°S

*Solomon Islands*

■ **Honiara**

*Guadalcanal*

## SOLOMON ISLANDS

165°E

*Banks Islands*

10°S

Scale 1:20 000 000
(projection: Lambert Azimuthal Equal Area)

0 kms      400      800      1 200

1 cm on the map represents 200 kms on the ground

5

90

4

Cooktown

Cairns

*Mitchell*

*Great Barrier Reef*

*Great Dividing Range*

Townsville

Charters Towers

Mackay

Clermont

Rockhampton

keetown

Cloncurry

*Coral Sea*

*Espíritu Santo*

## VANUATU

New Caledonia
(to France)

■ **Port Vila**

*Îles Loyauté*

170°E

175°E

180°

**FIJI**

Lautoka

*Viti Levu*

■ **Suva**

*Lau Group*

15°S

**QUEENSLAND**

Longreach

**I A**

Charleville

Roma

Bundaberg

Cunnamulla

Toowoomba

*New Caledonia*

**Nouméa**

20°S

*Tropic of Capricorn*

180°

## PACIFIC OCEAN

arree

Bourke

*Darling*

**Brisbane** ◉

Surfers Paradise

Moree

Grafton

25°S

Tamworth

**NEW SOUTH WALES**

*Great Dividing Range*

Ivanhoe

Port Macquarie

*Lord Howe Island*

Newcastle

Parramatta

Mildura

**Sydney** ◉

Wollongong

Wagga Wagga

■ **Canberra**

AUSTRALIAN CAPITAL TERRITORY

△ Mount Kosciuszko 2228m

30°S

ham

**VICTORIA**

Bendigo

Cooma

Mount

**Melbourne** ◉

Traralgon

Gambier

Geelong

*Tasman Sea*

*Bass Strait*

35°S

Marrawah

Devonport

Launceston

**TASMANIA**

*Tasmania*

Hobart

**Auckland** ◉ Manurewa

*North Island*

Hamilton

Rotorua

New Plymouth

*Lake Taupo*

### Key

**Elevation**

4 000 m
2 000 m
1 000 m
500 m
250 m
100 m
0
250 m
2 000 m
4 000 m

Below sea level

△ mountain

**Settlements**

◉ over 1 million

◎ 500 000 to 1 million

■ ◉ 100 000 to 500 000

■ ○ below 100 000

A red square indicates a national capital

145°E

150°E

155°E

45°S

## NEW ZEALAND

Palmerston North

Hastings

**Wellington** ■

*Aoraki (Mt Cook) 3744m* △

*South Island*

*Southern Alps*

Christchurch

40°S

Invercargill

160°E

*Stewart Island*

165°E

170°E

Dunedin

45°S

67

F          G          H

E

E

92

# NORTH AMERICA POLITICAL

North America is dominated by the United States, the world's most powerful nation. Canada and Mexico are the two other largest countries. To the south, there are the islands of the Caribbean and the narrow neck of land in Central America, which is divided into many smaller nations.

## Key

- ■ capital city

The Statue of Liberty was a gift of international friendship from France to the United States. Dedicated in 1886, it is a powerful symbol of democracy.

## Greenland

Greenland, the world's largest island, lies on the eastern edge of North America. Most of the land is covered by a thick ice sheet which has been left over from the last Ice Age. Only around 50 000 people live in Greenland, the majority of whom are Inuit.

Scale 1:49 000 000

0 kms   500   1 000   1 500   2 000

# NORTH AMERICA PHYSICAL

North America stretches from the Arctic to the Tropics. To the west, the Rockies form a high mountain chain and a barrier to climate and communications. To the east, the Great Plains are a vast area of flat land drained by the Mississippi river. The Great Lakes, on the border between the United States and Canada, are another key feature, which were created by glaciers in the last Ice Age.

## NORTH AMERICA FACTS

**HIGHEST MOUNTAIN:** Mount McKinley 6194 m

**LONGEST RIVER:** Mississippi/Missouri 6019 km

**BIGGEST LAKE:** Lake Superior 82414 sq km

**BIGGEST ISLAND:** Greenland 2166086 sq km

**BIGGEST DESERT:** Great Basin desert 492000 sq km

**BIGGEST COUNTRY:** Canada 9970610 sq km

**SMALLEST COUNTRY:** Saint Kitts & Nevis 269 sq km

### Key

**Elevation**

4 000 m
2 000 m
1 000 m
500 m
250 m
100 m
0
250 m — Below sea level
2 000 m
4 000 m

△ mountain
◬ volcano
▽ depression

**Scale 1:49 000 000**

0 kms 500 1 000 1 500 2 000

### Map labels

ASIA
Bering Strait
Bering Sea
Aleutian Islands
Aleutian Range
Brooks Range
Yukon
Gulf of Alaska
Alaska Range
△ Mount McKinley 6194m
Beaufort Sea
Coast Range
Great Bear Lake
Great Slave Lake
Canadian
ROCKY MOUNTAINS
Coast Mountains
Mount Rainier 4392m
◬ Mount St Helens 2549m
Coast Ranges
Sierra Nevada
Great Basin
Great Salt Lake
Death Valley -86 m ▽
Colorado Basin
Sonoran Desert
Lower California
Gulf of California
Sierra Madre Occidental
Sierra Madre Oriental
Rio Grande
Volcán Pico de Orizaba 5700m ◬
Yucatan Peninsula
Gulf of Mexico
Mississippi Delta
PACIFIC OCEAN
Great Plains
Missouri
Arkansas
Mississippi
Ohio
Great Shield
Hudson Bay
Laurentian Mountains
Lake Winnipeg
Lake Superior
Lake Huron
Lake Michigan
Lake Erie
Lake Ontario
Great Lakes
St. Lawrence
Appalachian Mountains
△ Brasstown Bald 1458m
Cape Cod
Nova Scotia
Newfoundland
Labrador Sea
Labrador
Baffin Island
Baffin Bay
Davis Strait
Hudson Strait
Arctic Circle
Greenland
ATLANTIC OCEAN
Tropic of Cancer
Cuba
Hispaniola
West Indies
Greater Antilles
Lesser Antilles
Caribbean Sea
Lake Nicaragua
Panama Canal
Isthmus of Panama
SOUTH AMERICA

Extremely broad and powerful, the Niagara Falls are situated between lakes Erie and Ontario. Until hydro-electric plants were set up, the water cut the falls back by 4 to 5 feet every year.

## DISCUSSION

How many North American countries lie within the Tropics?

Does Canada or the United States have the more varied landscape?

# NORTH AMERICA FROM THE SKY

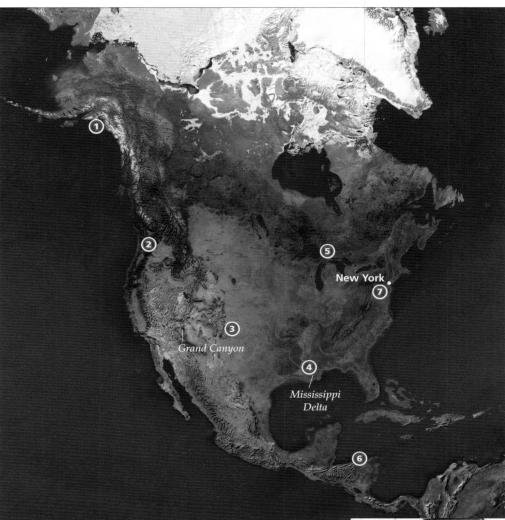

## Environmental hotspots

**1** Oil spill, Exxon Valdez, Alaska 1989

**2** Eruption, Mount St Helens, USA 1980

**3** Dust bowl disaster, USA 1930s

**4** Hurricane Katrina, New Orleans, USA 2005

**5** Acid rain, Great Lakes ongoing

**6** Hurricane Mitch, Nicaragua/Honduras 1998

**7** Nuclear accident, Three Mile Island, USA 1979

The arid areas in the southwest of the United States and Rocky Mountains are shown in brown in this satellite image. Further north and east, the prairies give way to forests. The Arctic Ocean and Greenland are covered by ice.

*Grand Canyon*

*Mississippi Delta*

New York

## USA at night

This night image reveals the pattern of cities and settlements across the United States. Note how strings of lights along the highways link some of the main towns and cities.

## Hurricane damage, Honduras

October 1998

Over 20000 people died and 3 million people were affected when Hurricane Mitch struck Nicaragua and Honduras. Although there were ferocious winds, the rain caused even greater problems as the storm was unusually slow-moving.

## New York

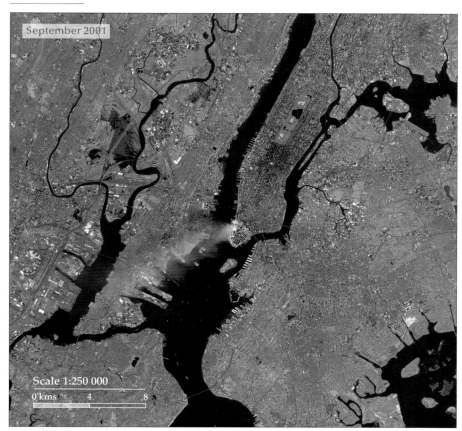

September 2001

Scale 1:250 000
0 kms    4    8

This image provides an aerial view of the buildings, waterways and open space in New York. It was taken soon after the terrorist attacks on the Twin Towers. Smoke can be seen drifting across the central district.

## Mississippi delta

Gulf of Mexico

May 2001

When the Mississippi river reaches the sea, strong currents cause sediments to create a 'bird's foot' delta. The shape of the delta is constantly changing as new channels form and others become blocked. This causes problems for shipping.

## Grand Canyon, Colorado River

June 2004

Scale 1:800 000
0 kms    10    20

The Grand Canyon is a World Heritage Site famous for its landscape, geology and wildlife. This infra-red image was taken in early summer. Vegetation is shown in red, forests in brown and bare rock in grey.

## Winter snowstorms

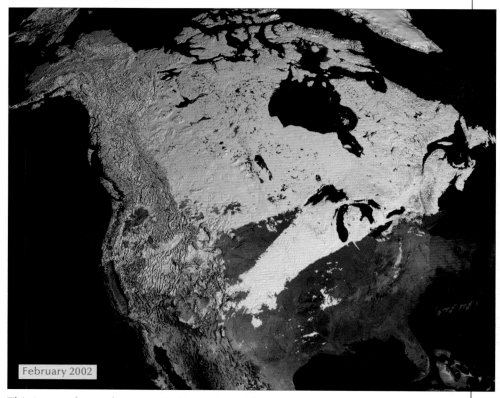

February 2002

This image shows the areas that have been hit by snowstorms. In the west of the United States, people depend on melting snow for most of their water. Satellites can help to monitor weather events.

# CANADA AND GREENLAND

Canada is the world's second largest country and has by far the longest coastline. Most people live in the south near the border with the USA. Here the climate is less severe than elsewhere. Further north, huge expanses of coniferous forest dotted with lakes eventually lead to the frozen lands around the Arctic Ocean. The Rockies are a high mountain chain along the western seaboard.

This moraine lake in the Rocky Mountains, Alberta is popular with hikers. An illustration of the lake appears on the back of the Canadian dollar bill or banknote.

## Key

### Elevation

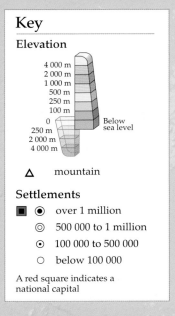

4 000 m
2 000 m
1 000 m
500 m
250 m
100 m
0
250 m       Below
2 000 m     sea level
4 000 m

△   mountain

### Settlements

■ ◉   over 1 million
◎   500 000 to 1 million
⊙   100 000 to 500 000
○   below 100 000

A red square indicates a national capital

ARCTIC OCEAN

Queen Elizabeth Islands
Axel Heib Island
Ellef Ringnes Island
Isachsen
Prince Patrick Island
Mould Bay
Parry Islands
Melville Island
Bathurst Island
Resolute
Some Islar
Prince of Wales Island
Viscount Melville Sound
McClintock Channel
Boot Penin
Beaufort Sea
Banks Island
Amundsen Gulf
Holman
Victoria Island
Cambridge Bay
Kugluktuk
Arctic Circle
Inuvik
Fort Good Hope
Mackenzie Mountains
ALASKA (part of USA)
YUKON TERRITORY
Great Bear Lake
Echo Bay
NUNAVU
Burnside
Back
Garry Lake
Dubawnt Lake
NORTHWEST TERRITORIES
Mount Logan 5959m
Tungsten
Yellowknife
Whitehorse
Gulf of Alaska
Watson Lake
Great Slave Lake
Fort Smith
Ca
Ar
140°W
Lake Athabasca
BRITISH COLUMBIA
C     A     N     A
Ch
Williston Lake
Fort St John
SASKATCHEWAN
Reindeer Lake
Fox Mine
PACIFIC OCEAN
Prince Rupert
Queen Charlotte Islands
Prince George
ALBERTA
Buffalo Narrows
MANIT
North Saskatchewan
The Pas
Queen Charlotte Sound
Mount Waddington 4016m
Mount Robson 3954m
Leduc
Saskatchewan
Lak
Win
Port Hardy
Kamloops
Red Deer
Saskatoon
Lake Manitoba
Vancouver Island
Kelowna
Calgary
Regina
Winn
Vancouver
Victoria
Lethbridge
Brandon
UNITED     STATES     OF     AMERIC

Coast Mountains
ROCKY  MOUNTAINS

80°N
70°N
60°N
50°N
140°W
130°W
120°W
110°W
100°W
90°W
80°

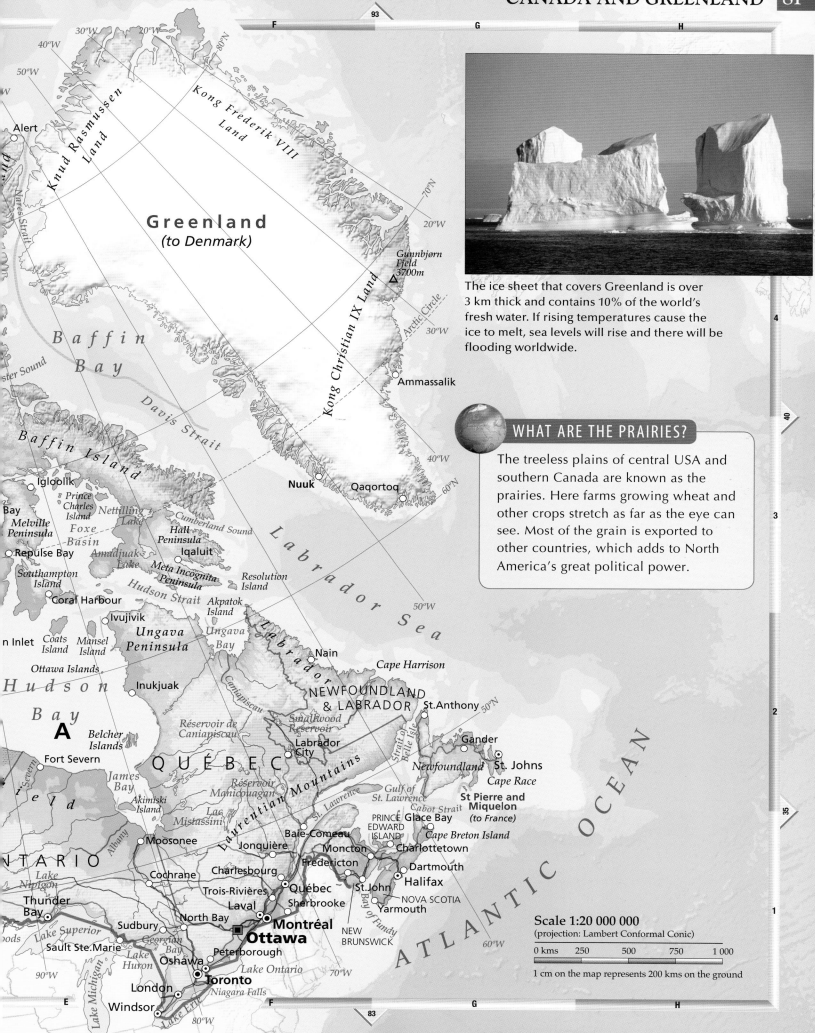

The ice sheet that covers Greenland is over 3 km thick and contains 10% of the world's fresh water. If rising temperatures cause the ice to melt, sea levels will rise and there will be flooding worldwide.

## WHAT ARE THE PRAIRIES?

The treeless plains of central USA and southern Canada are known as the prairies. Here farms growing wheat and other crops stretch as far as the eye can see. Most of the grain is exported to other countries, which adds to North America's great political power.

**Scale 1:20 000 000**
(projection: Lambert Conformal Conic)

| 0 kms | 250 | 500 | 750 | 1 000 |

1 cm on the map represents 200 kms on the ground

### Map labels

Greenland (to Denmark)

Knud Rasmussen Land
Kong Frederik VIII Land
Kong Christian IX Land
Alert
Gunnbjørn Fjeld 3700m
Arctic Circle
Ammassalik
Baffin Bay
Davis Strait
Nuuk
Qaqortoq
Baffin Island
Igloolik
Prince Charles Island
Nettilling Lake
Cumberland Sound
Bay
Melville Peninsula
Foxe Basin
Hall Peninsula
Iqaluit
Repulse Bay
Amadjuak Lake
Meta Incognita Peninsula
Resolution Island
Southampton Island
Hudson Strait
Akpatok Island
Coral Harbour
Ivujivik
Ungava Peninsula
Ungava Bay
Labrador Sea
Inlet
Coats Island
Mansel Island
Ottawa Islands
Inukjuak
Nain
Cape Harrison
Hudson Bay
A
Belcher Islands
Fort Severn
Caniapiscau
NEWFOUNDLAND & LABRADOR
St.Anthony
James Bay
Réservoir de Caniapiscau
Smallwood Reservoir
Gander
Akimiski Island
Labrador City
Newfoundland
St. Johns
Cape Race
QUÉBEC
Réservoir Manicouagan
St. Lawrence
Gulf of St. Lawrence
St Pierre and Miquelon (to France)
Lac Mistassini
Laurentian Mountains
Cabot Strait
Glace Bay
Cape Breton Island
Moosonee
Baie-Comeau
PRINCE EDWARD ISLAND
Jonquière
Moncton
Charlottetown
ONTARIO
Cochrane
Charlesbourg
Fredericton
Dartmouth
Lake Nipigon
Trois-Rivières
Québec
St.John
Halifax
Thunder Bay
Laval
Sherbrooke
NOVA SCOTIA
Yarmouth
North Bay
Montréal
NEW BRUNSWICK
Sudbury
Ottawa
Bay of Fundy
Sault Ste.Marie
Georgian Bay
Peterborough
Lake Superior
Lake Huron
Oshawa
Lake Ontario
London
Toronto
Niagara Falls
Windsor
Lake Erie
Lake Michigan

ATLANTIC OCEAN

# THE UNITED STATES OF AMERICA

The USA is a federation of 50 states including Alaska and Hawai'i. It is the wealthiest nation in the world with great industrial cities on the seaboards and prosperous farmlands inland. Nearly half of the USA is drained by the Mississippi river.

The Grand Canyon in Arizona is one of the great natural wonders of the world. It has been created by the Colorado River, which has cut through the rocks to form a valley over 600 metres deep.

## Key

**Elevation**

4 000 m
2 000 m
1 000 m
500 m
250 m
100 m
0
250 m — Below sea level
2 000 m
4 000 m

**Settlements**

■ ◉ over 1 million
◎ 500 000 to 1 million
⊙ 100 000 to 500 000
○ below 100 000

A red square indicates a national capital

△ mountain      ⌂ volcano

A tornado snakes its way through rural Kansas after destroying a home. Kansas suffers more tornado damage than any other state in the USA.

## WHAT ARE TORNADOES?

Tornadoes are small but violent storms with a funnel that reaches from the base of the clouds to the earth below. These rotating winds can exceed 400 kph, causing terrible destruction. Tornadoes are found all over the world but they are particularly common in central USA. It is thought they are caused by the mixing of cold and warm air in late spring and early summer.

Scale 1:13 000 000
(projection: Lambert Conformal Conic)

0 kms    200    400    600    800

1 cm on the map represents 130 kms on the ground

# CENTRAL AMERICA AND THE CARIBBEAN

A chain of high mountains, many of them volcanic, forms the spine of Central America. Mexico, with a population of over 100 million, is far larger than any of the other countries in the region. In the Caribbean, there are many small tropical islands that have become a popular destination for tourists from Europe and North America.

The Mayan civilisation originated in the Yucatan Peninsula, Mexico. This photograph shows the Temple of Warriors in the ruined city of Chichen Itza. It was built 1100–1300AD and is now an important tourist attraction.

Founded in 1325 at a height of over 2 000 metres, Mexico City has grown into a great metropolis. The Angel of Independence monument stands at the heart of the city.

83

E F G H

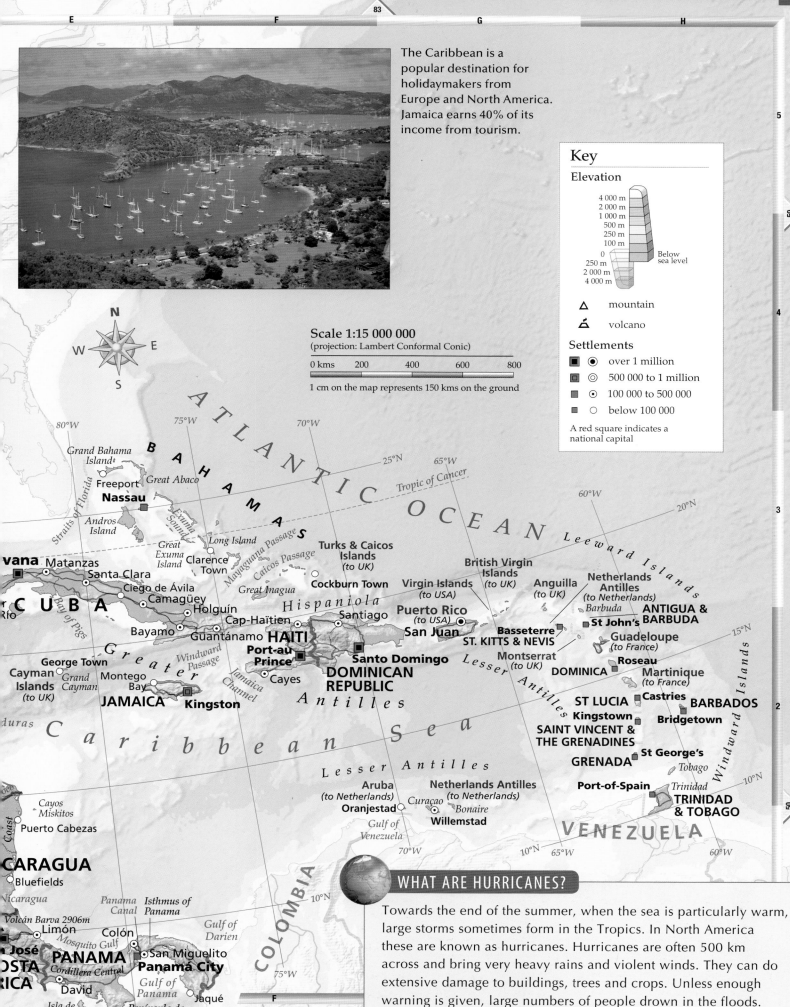

The Caribbean is a popular destination for holidaymakers from Europe and North America. Jamaica earns 40% of its income from tourism.

## Key

### Elevation

4 000 m
2 000 m
1 000 m
500 m
250 m
100 m
0
250 m
2 000 m
4 000 m

Below sea level

△ mountain

⛰ volcano

### Settlements

▪ ⦿ over 1 million

▣ ◎ 500 000 to 1 million

◼ ⊙ 100 000 to 500 000

◾ ○ below 100 000

A red square indicates a national capital

### Scale 1:15 000 000
(projection: Lambert Conformal Conic)

0 kms 200 400 600 800

1 cm on the map represents 150 kms on the ground

N
NW NE
W E
SW SE
S

A T L A N T I C   O C E A N

B A H A M A S

Grand Bahama Island
Freeport
**Nassau**
Great Abaco
Andros Island
Great Exuma Island
Long Island
Clarence Town
Exuma Sound
Great Inagua

Straits of Florida

25°N
Tropic of Cancer
65°W
60°W
20°N

Mayaguana Passage
Caicos Passage
Turks & Caicos Islands (to UK)
Cockburn Town

Leeward Islands

**vana** Matanzas
Santa Clara
Ciego de Ávila
Camagüey
Holguín
Bayamo
Guantánamo
C U B A
Río
Bay of Pigs

Hispaniola
Cap-Haïtien
Santiago
**HAITI**
**Port-au-Prince**
Cayes

Virgin Islands (to USA)
Puerto Rico (to USA)
San Juan

British Virgin Islands (to UK)
Anguilla (to UK)
Netherlands Antilles (to Netherlands)
Barbuda
**ANTIGUA & BARBUDA**
St John's
**Basseterre**
**ST. KITTS & NEVIS**
Montserrat (to UK)
Guadeloupe (to France)

George Town
Cayman Islands (to UK)
Grand Cayman
Montego Bay
**JAMAICA**
**Kingston**

Windward Passage
Jamaica Channel

Greater Antilles

**Santo Domingo**
**DOMINICAN REPUBLIC**

Lesser Antilles

Roseau
**DOMINICA**
Martinique (to France)

A n t i l l e s

C a r i b b e a n   S e a

**ST LUCIA**
Castries
**BARBADOS**
**Kingstown**
Bridgetown
**SAINT VINCENT & THE GRENADINES**
**GRENADA**
St George's
Tobago

Windward Islands

15°N

Lesser Antilles

Aruba (to Netherlands)
**Oranjestad**
Curaçao
Netherlands Antilles (to Netherlands)
Bonaire
**Willemstad**

Gulf of Venezuela

**Port-of-Spain**
Trinidad
**TRINIDAD & TOBAGO**

V E N E Z U E L A

10°N
70°W
65°W
60°W

**CARAGUA**
Bluefields
Nicaragua

Cayos Miskitos
Puerto Cabezas
Coast

Volcán Barva 2906m
**Limón**
**Colón**
Mosquito Gulf
**José**
**PANAMA**
**OSTA**
**RICA**
**David**
Isla de Coiba

Panama Canal
Isthmus of Panama
Gulf of Darien
10°N

**San Miguelito**
**Panamá City**
Cordillera Central
Gulf of Panama
Jaqué
Peninsula de Azuero

C O L O M B I A

75°W
80°W

🌍 **WHAT ARE HURRICANES?**

Towards the end of the summer, when the sea is particularly warm, large storms sometimes form in the Tropics. In North America these are known as hurricanes. Hurricanes are often 500 km across and bring very heavy rains and violent winds. They can do extensive damage to buildings, trees and crops. Unless enough warning is given, large numbers of people drown in the floods.

80°W 75°W 70°W

# SOUTH AMERICA POLITICAL

There are 12 independent countries in South America, plus French Guiana is governed by France. Brazil is by far the largest country, covering about half the continent and containing half of South America's population. Once a Portuguese colony, the official language in Brazil is Portuguese. Elsewhere Spanish is the main language, again reflecting historical links.

## The Falkland Islands (Islas Malvinas)

The Falkland Islands are 500 km off the coast of Argentina. Originally uninhabited, they attracted settlers from France, Spain, Britain and other countries. In 1982, a dispute between Argentina and the UK led to war. Both countries still claim ownership.

### Key

■ capital city
□ dependency capital city

Many of the people who live in South America are of mixed ancestry. The Amerindians were the first inhabitants, but many Europeans have also made it their home.

Scale 1:37 000 000

0 kms    500    1 000    1 500

# SOUTH AMERICA PHYSICAL

The longest mountain chain in the world, the Andes, runs down the western edge of South America. From here, the Amazon flows eastwards through rainforests and grasslands to the Atlantic Ocean. South America narrows as it approaches Antarctica. Cape Horn at the southern tip is famous for cold winds and turbulent waves.

Scale 1:41 000 000

0 kms    500    1 000    1 500

## SOUTH AMERICA FACTS

**HIGHEST MOUNTAIN:** Cerro Aconcagua  6 959 m

**LONGEST RIVER:** Amazon  6 530 km

**BIGGEST LAKE:** Lake Titicaca, Bolivia/Peru  8 547 sq km

**BIGGEST ISLAND:** Tierra del Fuego  48 100 sq km

**BIGGEST DESERT:** Patagonian desert  260 000 sq km

**BIGGEST COUNTRY:** Brazil  8 547 000 sq km

**SMALLEST COUNTRY:** Surinam  163 270 sq km

### Key

**Elevation**

4 000 m
2 000 m
1 000 m
500 m
250 m
100 m
0
250 m
2 000 m
4 000 m

Below sea level

△ mountain
⌂ volcano
▽ depression

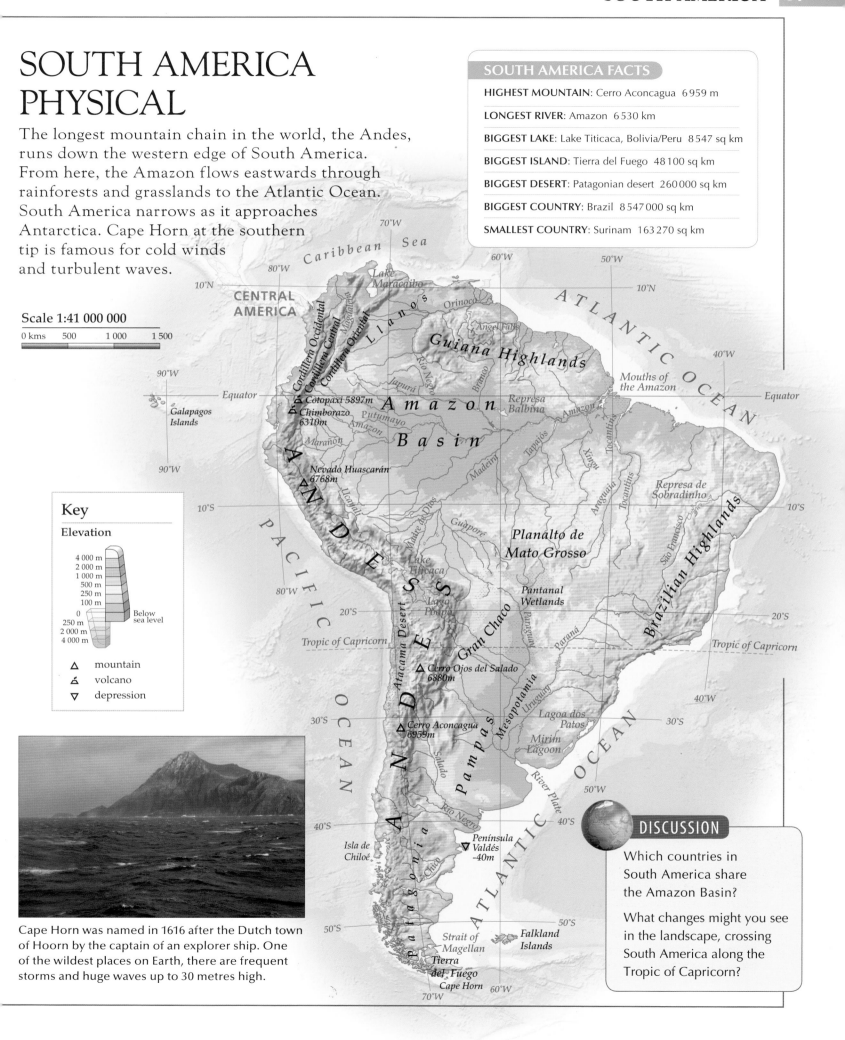

Cape Horn was named in 1616 after the Dutch town of Hoorn by the captain of an explorer ship. One of the wildest places on Earth, there are frequent storms and huge waves up to 30 metres high.

## DISCUSSION

Which countries in South America share the Amazon Basin?

What changes might you see in the landscape, crossing South America along the Tropic of Capricorn?

# SOUTH AMERICA FROM THE SKY

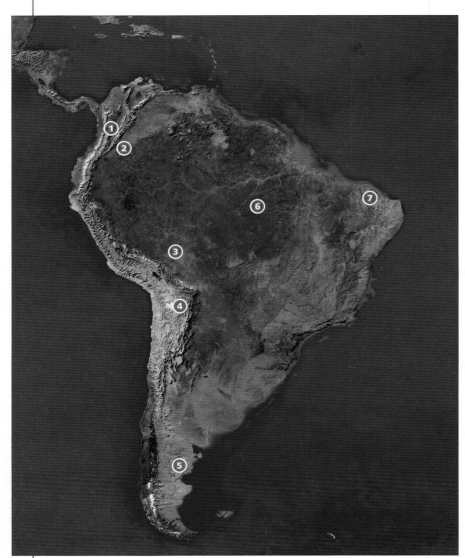

## Environmental hotspots

**1** Mudslide, Nevado del Ruiz, Colombia 1984

**2** Deforestation and soil loss, cocaine farming, Colombia ongoing

**3** Forest fires, Amazon rainforest ongoing

**4** Air, water and land pollution, Cerro Rico mine, Bolivia ongoing

**5** Ozone hole, Patagonia, Argentina, 1980s onwards

**6** Illegal logging, Amazon ongoing

**7** Drought, northeast Brazil ongoing

In this image, the Amazon Basin is shown in dark green and the Andes in brown. Notice how some of the peaks are capped with snow, especially towards Antarctica.

## South America at night

The pattern of light blue dots shows the main cities in Brazil, Argentina and the northwest. The coastline and country boundaries have been picked out in red in this image.

## Cerro Rico mine, Bolivia

c.1995

The Cerro Rico mines have been producing silver and tin for hundreds of years, but now the minerals have almost been exhausted. Metal pollution now contaminates the soil and river water in the surrounding area.

## Brasilia

1995

Brasilia was created as the brand new capital of Brazil in 1960. In this false colour image the buildings and streets are light blue, woods are brown and lakes deep blue. As Brasilia grows larger, the buildings are extending further and further into the countryside.

## Glaciers, Argentina

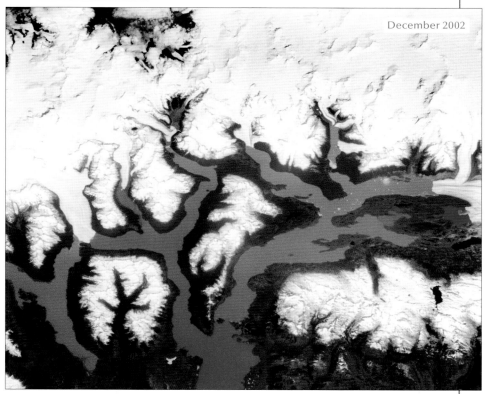

December 2002

These glaciers form part of an ice field in southern Argentina. As the ice melts, the water flows into a lake. The melt water, which is heavy in sediments, shows up in light blue in this photograph. The glaciers in this region are now retreating steadily, perhaps due to global warming.

## Clearing the rainforest

September 2002

BRAZIL

Iguaçu River

ARGENTINA

The impact of human activity is shown very clearly in this photograph. To the south of the Iguaçu river, the land has been cleared for agriculture. To the north, the rainforest remains untouched. People have different opinions about the benefits of these changes.

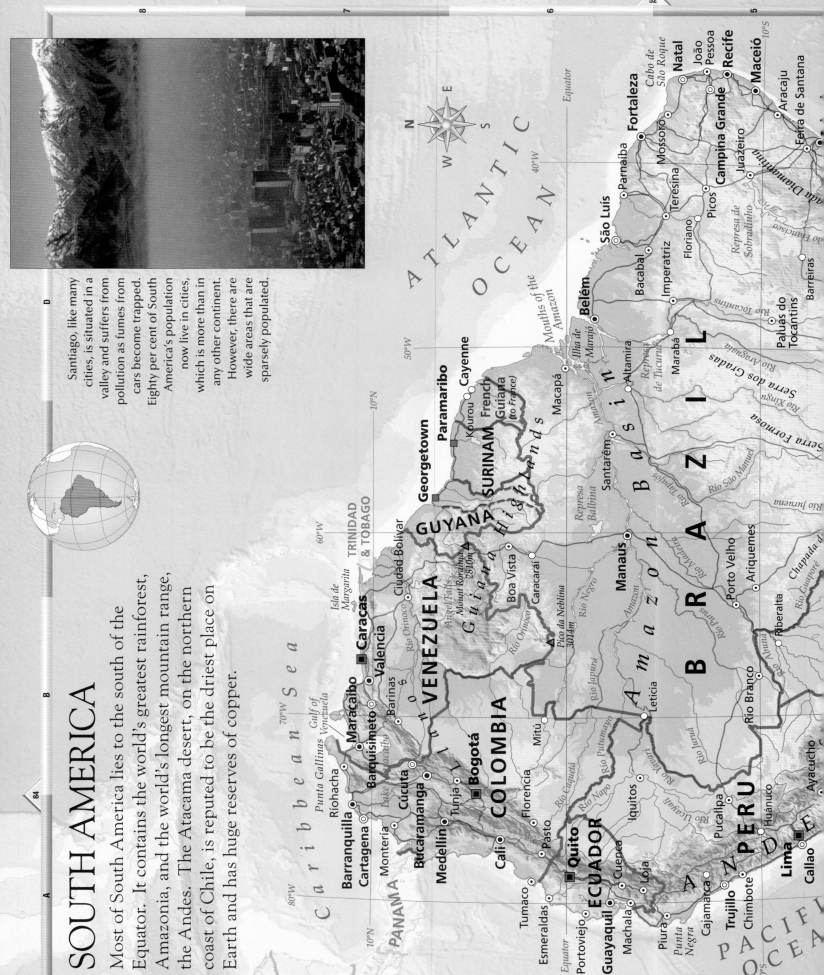

# SOUTH AMERICA

Most of South America lies to the south of the Equator. It contains the world's greatest rainforest, Amazonia, and the world's longest mountain range, the Andes. The Atacama desert, on the northern coast of Chile, is reputed to be the driest place on Earth and has huge reserves of copper.

Santiago, like many cities, is situated in a valley and suffers from pollution as fumes from cars become trapped. Eighty per cent of South America's population now live in cities, which is more than in any other continent. However, there are wide areas that are sparsely populated.

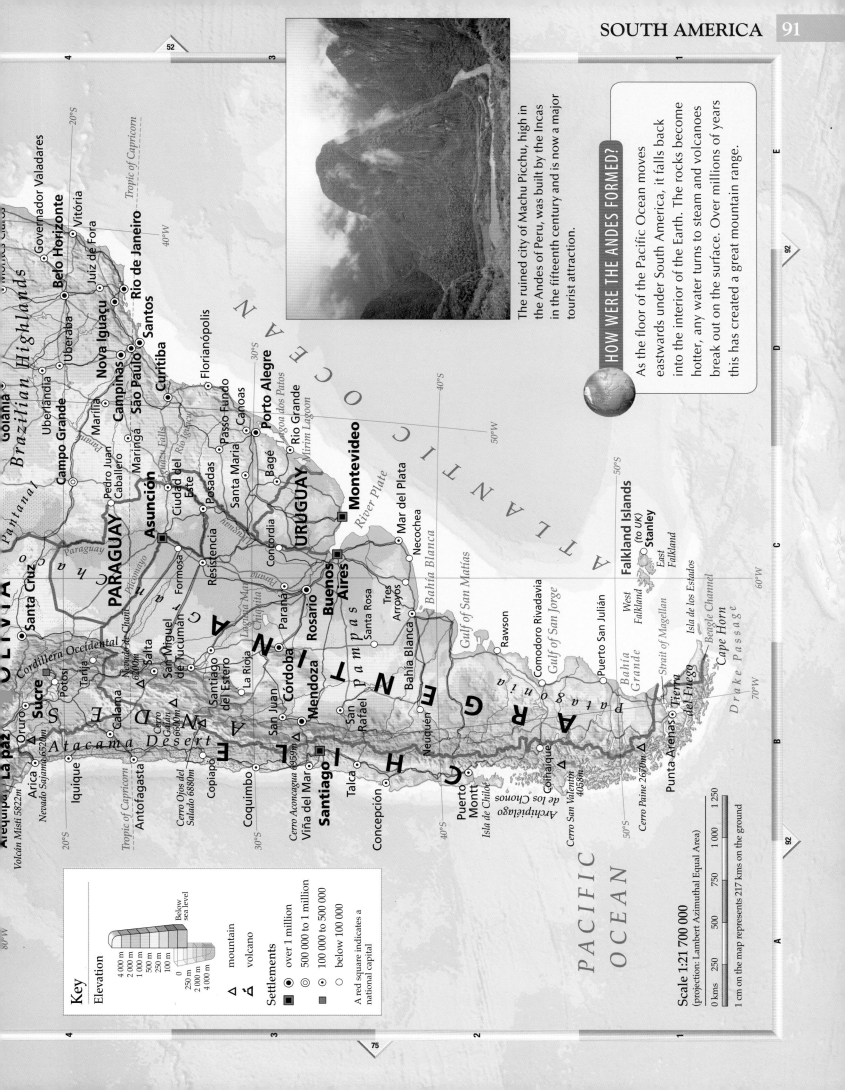

The ruined city of Machu Picchu, high in the Andes of Peru, was built by the Incas in the fifteenth century and is now a major tourist attraction.

## HOW WERE THE ANDES FORMED?

As the floor of the Pacific Ocean moves eastwards under South America, it falls back into the interior of the Earth. The rocks become hotter, any water turns to steam and volcanoes break out on the surface. Over millions of years this has created a great mountain range.

Scale 1:21 700 000
(projection: Lambert Azimuthal Equal Area)

0 kms   250   500   750   1 000   1 250

1 cm on the map represents 217 kms on the ground

### Key

**Elevation**

4 000 m
2 000 m
1 000 m
500 m
250 m
100 m
0
250 m
2 000 m
4 000 m
Below sea level

△ mountain
△ volcano

**Settlements**

◉ over 1 million
◎ 500 000 to 1 million
● 100 000 to 500 000
○ below 100 000

A red square indicates a national capital

# ANTARCTICA

Antarctica is the fifth largest continent. Surrounded by oceans and covered by a great sheet of ice up to 3 000 metres thick, it is the last great wilderness on Earth. In winter, pack ice forms round the coast, doubling the size of the continent. The intense cold helps to drive the world's climate.

### Key

ice sheet covering land

△ mountain
⌂ volcano
● research station

0
250 m
2 000 m
4 000 m — sea depth

◇ ◇ ◇ limit of winter pack ice
⋯⋯⋯ limit of summer pack ice

### Antarctic exploration

●●●● Ernest Shackleton (British) 1907-8
●●●● Roald Amundsen (Norwegian) 1910-1[?]
●●●● Robert Scott (British) 1910-13
●●●● British Commonwealth Transantarctic 1958

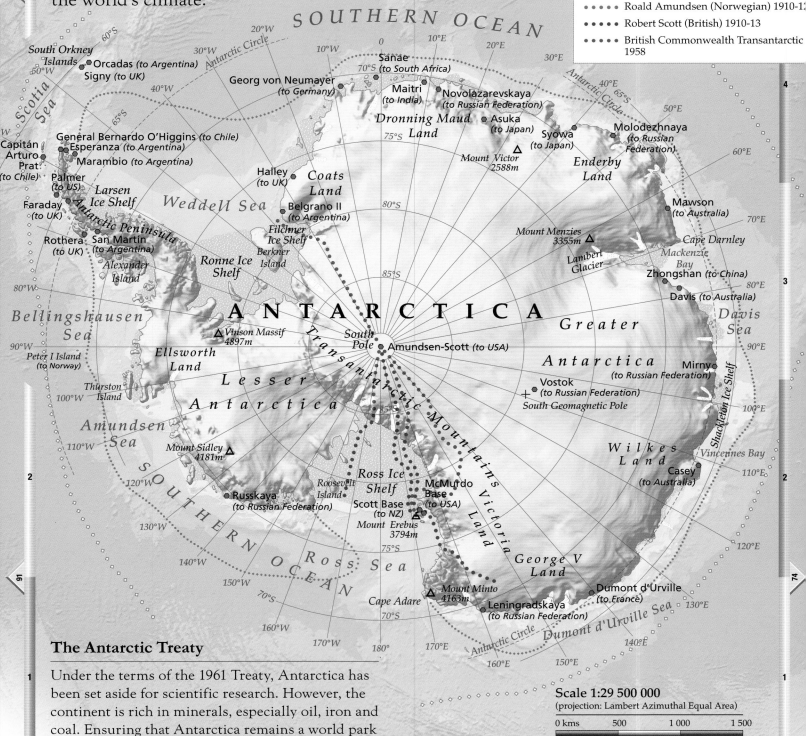

### The Antarctic Treaty

Under the terms of the 1961 Treaty, Antarctica has been set aside for scientific research. However, the continent is rich in minerals, especially oil, iron and coal. Ensuring that Antarctica remains a world park is one of the challenges for the future.

**Scale 1:29 500 000**
(projection: Lambert Azimuthal Equal Area)

0 kms          500          1 000          1 500

1 cm on the map represents 295 kms on the ground

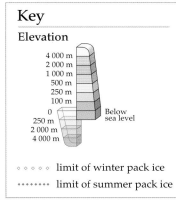

# THE ARCTIC

Whereas Antarctica is a major land mass, the Arctic consists of a relatively shallow ocean. In summer, the water attracts whales, seals and other creatures searching for food. In winter the cold increases and pack ice extends southwards across the Arctic Circle.

### Key

**Elevation**

4 000 m
2 000 m
1 000 m
500 m
250 m
100 m
0
250 m
2 000 m
4 000 m

Below sea level

◇ ◇ ◇ ◇ ◇ limit of winter pack ice

•••••••• limit of summer pack ice

## Rising temperatures

Scientists are now concerned that polar temperatures are rising too fast. As well as causing the ice to melt, this threatens the tundra. Great quantities of carbon dioxide (one of the greenhouse gases) could be released as the tundra of northern Russia and Canada begins to thaw.

**Scale 1:46 000 000**
(projection: Lambert Azimuthal Equal Area)

0 kms          1 000          2 000

1cm on the map represents 460 kms on the ground

### DISCUSSION

What are the main differences between the Arctic and Antarctic?

Do you think Antarctica should be preserved as a wilderness?

# WORLD DEVELOPMENT

Development is about improving the quality of people's lives. This involves not only helping them to become richer, but also seeing that they stay healthy, have the chance to learn new things and fulfil their potential as human beings. As human numbers go on rising, we need to ensure that we share the Earth's resources fairly and use them sustainably.

> *"We must recognise that our common humanity is more important than our differences."*
>
> Bill Clinton
> President of the United States 1993-2001

## Differences in development

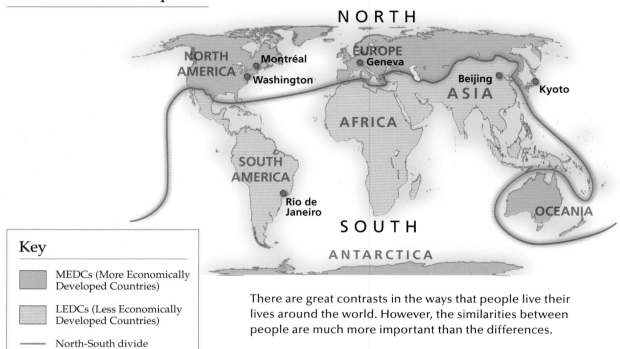

There are great contrasts in the ways that people live their lives around the world. However, the similarities between people are much more important than the differences.

### Key

| | |
|---|---|
| ▨ | MEDCs (More Economically Developed Countries) |
| ▧ | LEDCs (Less Economically Developed Countries) |
| —— | North-South divide |

## The world family

Find out more about the human family from this illustration. The figures tell you how many of us would belong to each group if there were only 100 people in the world.

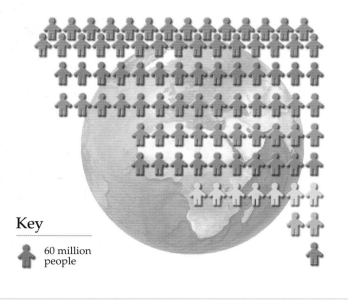

**29** are under 15 years old

**14** do not have enough to eat

**14** are unable to read or write

**10** have a car

**10** use the Internet

**7** are over 65 years old

**2** have never been to school

**1** is a refugee or slave

### Key

🧍 60 million people

## International agreements

**Washington 1959**
Antarctic Treaty protects the natural environment

**Washington 1975**
Convention on International Trade in Endangered Species (CITES) attempts to protect wildlife

**Montréal 1987**
Montréal Protocol phases out CFCs and pollutants that damage the ozone layer

**Geneva 1989**
UN convention on the rights of the child

**Rio de Janeiro 1992**
Earth summit sets an environmental agenda for the 21st century

**Beijing 1995**
UN conference on human rights recognises the status of women

**Kyoto 1997**
Convention on climate change agrees international limits on carbon emissions

### DISCUSSION

What goals would you set to improve life in your own school or community?

On a global scale, do you think that the North-South divide is going to become more or less important in the future?

## Millennium Development Goals

In 2000, 189 member countries of the United Nations agreed on a set of goals to reduce poverty and improve people's lives around the world by 2015.

You can find out more about human welfare in the next few pages (96–105). As you make comparisons, remember that there are many inequalities within countries as well as between them.

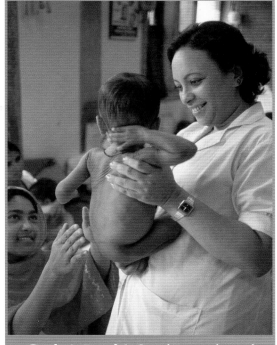

**Goals 4, 5 and 6** Cut the number of deaths from disease and childbirth.

**Goal 1** Eradicate extreme poverty and hunger.

**Goal 7** See that the environment is used sustainably.

**Goal 2** See that all children go to primary school.

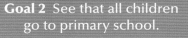

**Goal 3** Promote equality between men and women.

**Goal 8** Develop partnerships between nations.

# HEALTH

**Millennium development targets:**

- Reduce the number of children who die under the age of 5 by two-thirds
- Halt the spread of AIDS and malaria

In many parts of the world, people are living longer than they used to. People are healthier as a result of improvements in food and water supply. There are also more doctors and hospitals to help them when they fall sick. Around the world, rich people generally live longer than those who are poor. In eastern Europe and central Asia, economic problems have affected people's health. AIDS has led to a sharp fall in life expectancy in sub-Saharan Africa.

## Population pyramids

**❶ USA**

Life expectancy at birth (years)

Slight improvement

Source: State of the World's Children

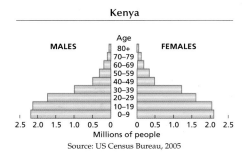

### Kenya

Source: US Census Bureau, 2005

There are many young people in Kenya as indicated by the triangular shape of this pyramid.

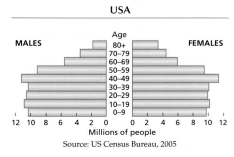

### USA

Source: US Census Bureau, 2005

This more regular profile suggests that the USA has an ageing population.

### Russian Federation

Source: US Census Bureau, 2005

The difference in the number of men and women over 60 is the result of the Second World War.

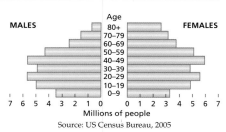

### China

Source: US Census Bureau, 2005

In China, the One Child Policy has led to a drop in the number of children under the age of 10.

**❺ Brazil**

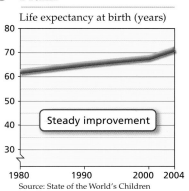

Life expectancy at birth (years)

Steady improvement

Source: State of the World's Children

## ➋ UK

**Life expectancy at birth (years)**

*Slight improvement*

Source: State of the World's Children

## ➌ Russian Federation

**Life expectancy at birth (years)**

*Problems in 1990s with break up of Soviet Union*

Source: State of the World's Children

Improvements in healthcare mean that this Chinese child can expect to live until the last decades of this century.

## ➍ China

**Life expectancy at birth (years)**

*Steady progress*

Source: State of the World's Children

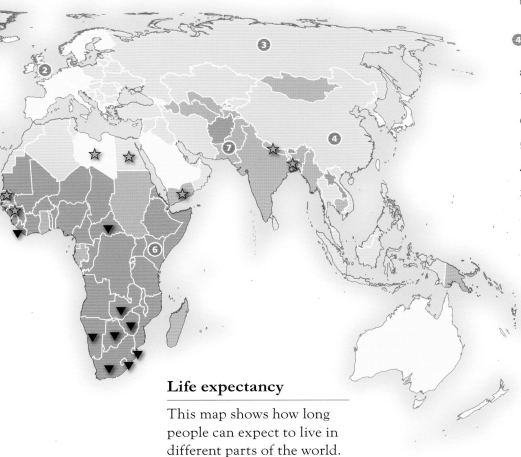

## Life expectancy

This map shows how long people can expect to live in different parts of the world.

### Key

**Life expectancy at birth in years**

- above 75
- 65 to 74
- 55 to 64
- below 55

**Change in life expectancy**

☆ countries where life expectancy has **increased** by 10 years or more since 1990

▼ countries where life expectancy has **decreased** by 10 years or more since 1990

Source: State of the World's Children 1992, 2006

## ➏ Kenya

**Life expectancy at birth (years)**

*AIDS takes its toll*

Source: State of the World's Children

## ➐ Pakistan

**Life expectancy (years)**

*Problems as Pakistan stays poor*

Source: State of the World's Children

## DISCUSSION

Which countries have had big increases or decreases in life expectancy?

What problems might increasing numbers of old people cause?

# WEALTH

## Millennium development target:
Halve the number of people earning less than $1 a day

The world's wealth is distributed unevenly. In every country there are some people who are very rich and others who are very poor. Globally, there are a few countries that are much richer than the rest. This leaves 80% of the world's population with less than 20% of the world's wealth.

## Wealth worldwide

This map shows differences in wealth between countries. It is based on GDP (gross domestic product) per head. The GDP is the total value of the goods and services a country produces in a year.

### Change in wealth

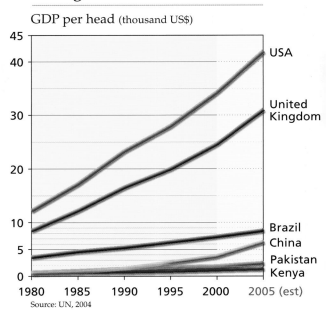

GDP per head (thousand US$)

Source: UN, 2004

Over the last 20 years, differences in wealth between nations have become steadily greater.

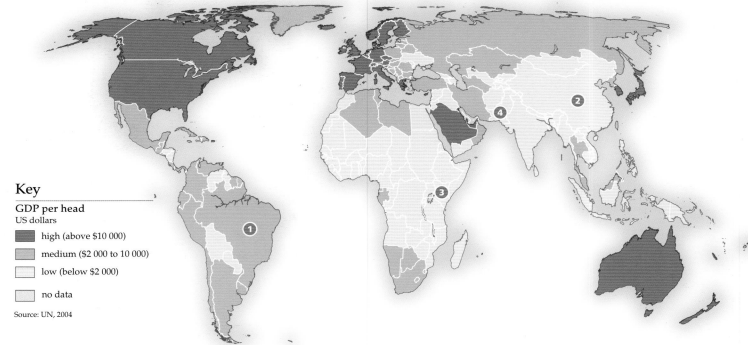

### Key
**GDP per head**
US dollars

- high (above $10 000)
- medium ($2 000 to 10 000)
- low (below $2 000)
- no data

Source: UN, 2004

**① Brazil**
Percentage of people earning below $1 a day
Source: UN, 2004

**② China**
Percentage of people earning below $1 a day
Source: UN, 2004

**③ Kenya**
Percentage of people earning below $1 a day
Source: UN, 2004

**④ Pakistan**
Percentage of people earning below $1 a day
Source: UN, 2004

# FOOD

Around the world some people have too much to eat, others have too little. Malnutrition has a particularly severe effect on young children. Not only are they weaker than adults, they can also suffer permanent brain damage if not properly fed. What happens in the first few years sets the stage for success in later life.

## Key

Daily calorie intake per person

- below 2000 – less than 90% of requirements
- 2000 to 2 500 – 90 to 100%
- 2 500 to 3 000 – 101 to 110%
- above 3 000 – over 110%
- no data
- ▼ countries where many young children are underweight

Source: Human Development Report, 2004

## World food consumption

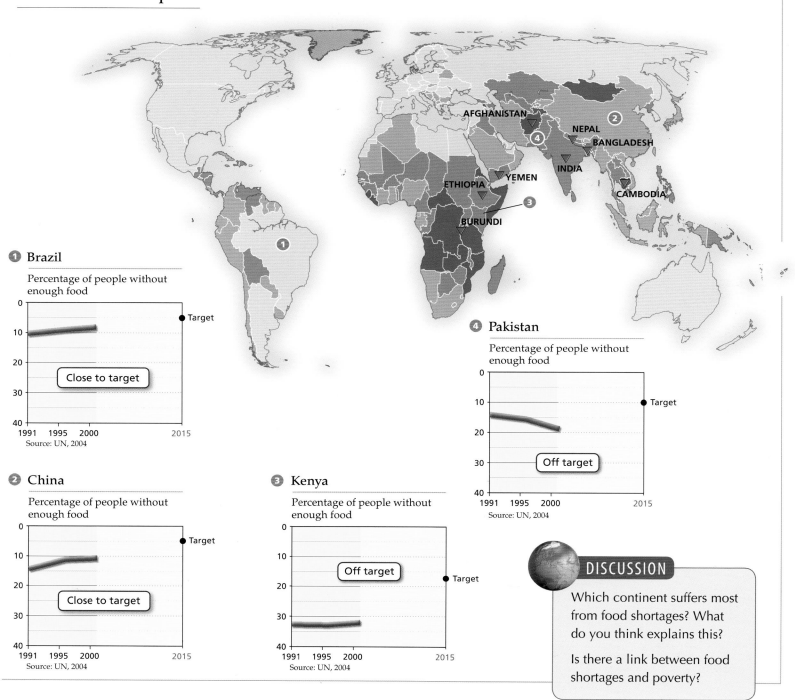

**AFGHANISTAN** ▼  **NEPAL** ▼  **BANGLADESH** ▼  **INDIA** ▼  **YEMEN** ▼  **CAMBODIA** ▼  **ETHIOPIA** ▼  **BURUNDI**  ② ④ ③ ①

**❶ Brazil**

Percentage of people without enough food

● Target

**Close to target**

1991  1995  2000    2015
Source: UN, 2004

**❹ Pakistan**

Percentage of people without enough food

● Target

**Off target**

1991  1995  2000    2015
Source: UN, 2004

**❷ China**

Percentage of people without enough food

● Target

**Close to target**

1991  1995  2000    2015
Source: UN, 2004

**❸ Kenya**

Percentage of people without enough food

**Off target**

● Target

1991  1995  2000    2015
Source: UN, 2004

**DISCUSSION**

Which continent suffers most from food shortages? What do you think explains this?

Is there a link between food shortages and poverty?

# EDUCATION

## Millennium development target:

Ensure that all children, boys and girls alike, finish their course at primary school

*"There is no single more effective anti-poverty strategy than education."*

Gordon Brown,
UK politician

In the modern world, it is essential to know how to read and write. Education also helps people to live more fulfilling lives. All over the world the number of pupils attending school is improving. However, 140 million children still have no access to education. Many of them live in south Asia and sub-Saharan Africa. Girls suffer more than boys as they are expected to do jobs around the house. This has an impact in later life. Educated women tend to have fewer children and look after their family better than those who have not been to school.

### Children in primary school

This map shows the percentage of children from different countries who have completed their primary education.

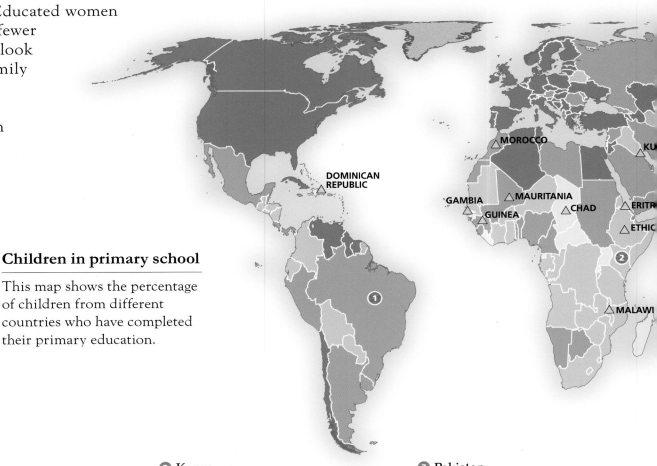

**1 Brazil**

Percentage of children completing primary school

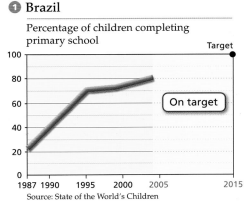

On target

Source: State of the World's Children

**2 Kenya**

Percentage of children completing primary school

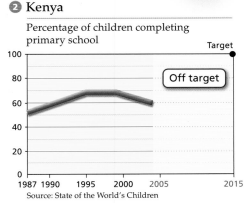

Off target

Source: State of the World's Children

**3 Pakistan**

Percentage of children completing primary school

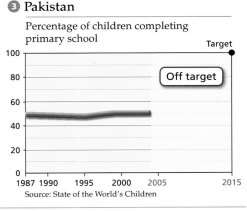

Off target

Source: State of the World's Children

## Differences between boys and girls

Average number of years schooling for boys and girls

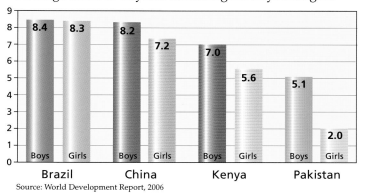

Source: World Development Report, 2006

In most countries, boys have priority for schooling.

## Differences between towns and villages

Average number of years schooling in urban and rural areas

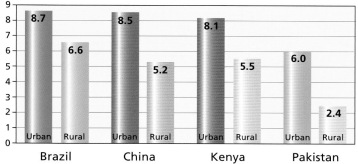

Source: World Development Report, 2006

Children living in urban areas have a better chance of going to school than those in rural areas.

### Key

**Children in primary school**
Percentage of children who have completed primary education

- above 95%
- 80 to 94%
- 50 to 79%
- below 50%
- no data

Source: State of the World's Children, 2005

△ countries where the number of children going to primary school has increased by 50% since 1990

## Adult illiteracy

Percentage of adult population who can read and write

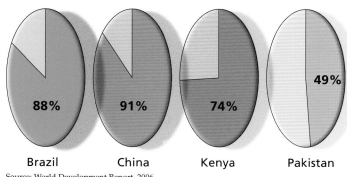

| Brazil | China | Kenya | Pakistan |

88%   91%   74%   49%

Source: World Development Report, 2006

There are 860 million illiterate adults worldwide – two-thirds of them are women.

### ④ China

Percentage of children completing primary school

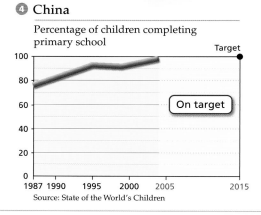

Target

On target

1987 1990 1995 2000 2005 2015

Source: State of the World's Children

## DISCUSSION

Why do you think children in LEDCs have a better chance of going to school in towns than in villages?

How would your life be affected if you were unable to read and write?

# ENVIRONMENT

**Millennium development target:**
Reverse the loss of environmental resources

Like all other living creatures, our survival depends on the natural environment. Water, air, food and fuel are essential for our daily lives. We also have to dispose of waste and rubbish. The amount of land needed to sustain us is known as our 'environmental footprint'.

The growth in human numbers and the increasing demand for resources mean our environmental footprint is growing heavier. We now use more resources each year than the Earth can naturally replace. Reversing this trend is a key challenge for the future.

> "The greatest challenge of ...our time... is to save the planet from destruction. It will require changing the very foundations of modern civilization – the relationship of humans to nature."
>
> Mikhail Gorbachev
> President of the Soviet Union 1985–1991

## World footprint

Number of Earth's required to support human activity

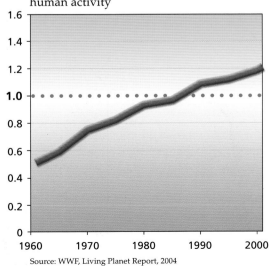

Since the mid 1980s the demands that people have placed on the Earth have exceeded its natural capacity.

Source: WWF, Living Planet Report, 2004

## Environmental footprints

This map shows the amount of land used by people in different countries.

### Key

Environmental footprint per person
(hectares per person)

- 5.0 to 10.0
- 3.0 to 4.9
- 1.5 to 2.9
- below 1.5

- no data

Source: WWF, Living Planet Report, 2004

### DISCUSSION

Is it fair that some countries have a much larger environmental footprint than others?

What could you do to reduce the size of your environmental footprint?

Renewable energy is one way of changing the demands we place on the environment. Cutting our consumption is also essential, especially in Europe and North America.

## Country footprints

In some countries, people make much bigger demands on the environment than others. These footprints were calculated by dividing the amount of land needed to provide what each country uses by its total population.

(hectares per person)
Source: WWF Living Planet Report, 2004

### Earth's capacity

(2.2 hectares per person)

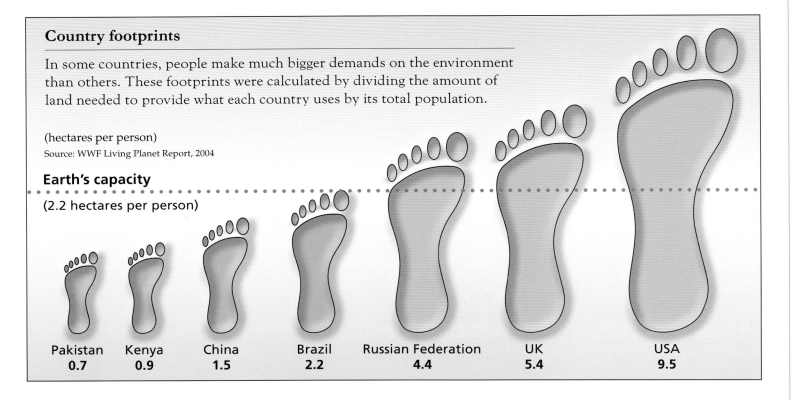

| Pakistan | Kenya | China | Brazil | Russian Federation | UK | USA |
|----------|-------|-------|--------|--------------------|-----|-----|
| 0.7 | 0.9 | 1.5 | 2.2 | 4.4 | 5.4 | 9.5 |

# WATER

## Millennium development target:

Halve the number of people without safe water and sanitation

Water is essential for our lives. We use it for drinking, washing, cooking and cleaning. In poor countries (LEDCs), obtaining clean water can be a problem. The people who live in shanty towns around big cities often have to make do with polluted supplies. In some parts of rural Africa and Asia, women spend many hours each day simply fetching and carrying water of often poor quality from a pump or well.

Eighty per cent of sickness and disease in LEDCs is caused by dirty water and poor sanitation. Nearly all these illnesses could be prevented. It would cost relatively little to bring safe water to everyone. This would help to save the lives of thousands of young children who die needlessly from waterborne diseases every day.

> *"No single measure would do more to reduce disease and save lives in the developing world than bringing safe water and adequate sanitation to all."*
>
> Kofi Annan, UN Secretary General

## Safe drinking water

This map shows the number of people who have access to clean water around the world.

### Key

**Access to clean drinking water**
(% of population)

- 90 to 100
- 75 to 89
- 50 to 74
- below 50
- no data

Source: UN, 2004

**Water disputes**

- ☆ conflict over access to water
- ⌁ disputed river

**BRAZIL, ARGEN**
*Paraná river*

It costs around £15 per person to provide safe water and sanitation in deprived areas. Everyone in the community benefits from the improvements.

**① Brazil**

Percentage of population with access to clean water

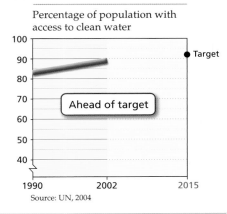

Ahead of target

Source: UN, 2004

## ② Russian Federation

Percentage of population with access to clean water

Ahead of target

Source: UN, 2004

## ③ China

Percentage of population with access to clean water

On target

Source: UN, 2004

## How much water do we use?

The amount of water used by in different countries around the world
(thousand litres per person in 2000)

Source: FAO

13 ................. Kenya

20 .................. China

40 ................ UK

67 ...................... Brazil

215 ..... USA

ISRAEL, SYRIA, JORDAN
*river and Sea of Galilee*

TURKEY, SYRIA, IRAQ
*Tigris, Euphrates rivers*

EGYPT, SUDAN, ETHIOPIA, UGANDA
*The Nile*

CHINA, LAOS, CAMBODIA, VIETNAM
*Mekong river*

## ④ Kenya

Percentage of population with access to clean water

On target

Source: UN, 2004

## ⑤ Pakistan

Percentage of population with access to clean water

Ahead of target

Source: UN, 2004

### DISCUSSION

Why do you think there are more and more demands on water resources?

Why do you think water supplies are usually worse in the country areas of LEDCs than in towns?

# HOW TO USE THIS INDEX

To find a place in the atlas first look up the name in the index. Next to the name you will see a page number and grid reference, e.g. Canary Islands **50 B4**. Use the page number to go to the correct page in the atlas, page **50** in this example. Next look along the bottom of the page to find the letter **B** and then at the side of the page to find the number **4**. You will find the Canary Islands where these two references meet.

The index also tells you the latitude and longitude of places, e.g. Canary Islands 50 B4 **28°0'N 15°30'W**. This reference is used to find the exact position of a place on the surface of the Earth. You can see how latitude and longitude works by looking at pages 4 and 5 of the atlas.

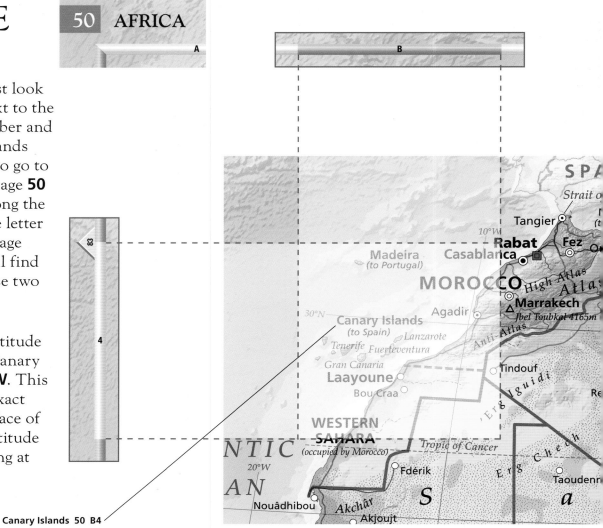

50 AFRICA

Canary Islands  50  B4

## A

| | | |
|---|---|---|
| Aalborg | 41 B2 | 57°3'N 9°56'E |
| Aberdeen | 34 D3 | 57°10'N 2°4'W |
| Aberystwyth | 33 B3 | 52°25'N 4°5'W |
| Abha | 61 E1 | 18°16'N 42°32'E |
| Abidjan | 50 C2 | 5°19'N 4°1'W |
| Abu Dhabi | 61 F2 | 24°30'N 54°20'E |
| Abuja | 50 D2 | 9°4'N 7°28'E |
| Acapulco | 84 B2 | 16°51'N 99°53'W |
| Accra | 50 C2 | 5°33'N 0°15'W |
| Achill Head | 35 B4 | 53°58'N 10°15'W |
| Aconcagua, Cerro | 91 B3 | 32°36'S 69°53'W |
| A Coruña | 42 C2 | 43°22'N 8°24'W |
| Adamawa Highlands | 50 D2 | 7°0'N 12°0'E |
| Adana | 60 D4 | 37°0'N 35°19'E |
| Addis Ababa | 51 G2 | 9°0'N 38°43'E |
| Adelaide | 74 D2 | 34°56'S 138°36'E |
| Aden | 61 E1 | 12°51'N 45°5'E |
| Aden, Gulf of | 51 H2 | 12°22'N 46°51'E |
| Adriatic Sea | 43 F2 | 43°32'N 14°34'E |
| Afghanistan | 58 C1 | 32°39'N 64°23'E |
| Agra | 63 E4 | 27°9'N 78°0'E |
| Ahaggar | 50 D3 | 23°54'N 6°23'E |
| Ahmadabad | 62 D3 | 23°3'N 72°40'E |
| Ahvaz | 61 F3 | 31°20'N 48°38'E |
| Aïr, Massif de l' | 50 D3 | 18°25'N 8°55'E |
| Akchâr | 50 B3 | 20°54'N 14°11'W |
| Akita | 67 F3 | 39°44'N 140°6'E |
| Aktau | 58 C2 | 43°37'N 51°14'E |
| Aktobe | 58 C3 | 50°18'N 57°10'E |
| Alabama | 83 G3 | 33°6'N 86°44'W |
| Alabama River | 83 G2 | 31°8'N 87°57'W |
| Aland Islands | 41 D3 | 60°14'N 19°54'E |
| Aland Sea | 41 D3 | 60°0'N 20°0'E |
| Alaska | 82 A4 | 65°0'N 150°0'W |
| Alaska, Gulf of | 80 B2 | 58°0'N 145°0'W |
| Albania | 45 A2 | 41°12'N 19°58'E |
| Albany, Australia | 74 C2 | 35°3'N 117°54'E |
| Albany, Canada | 81 E1 | 51°15'N 84°6'W |
| Alberta | 80 C2 | 55°33'N 114°38'W |
| Albert, Lake | 53 E5 | 1°41'N 30°55'E |
| Aldershot | 31 F3 | 51°15'N 0°47'W |
| Aleppo | 60 D4 | 36°14'N 37°10'E |
| Aleutian Islands | 82 A3 | 52°0'N 176°0'W |

| | | |
|---|---|---|
| Alexandria | 51 F4 | 31°7'N 29°51'E |
| Al Fujayrah | 61 G3 | 25°9'N 56°18'E |
| Algeria | 50 C4 | 28°4'N 0°45'E |
| Algiers | 50 D5 | 36°47'N 2°58'E |
| Al Hufuf | 61 F3 | 25°21'N 49°34'E |
| Alice Springs | 74 D3 | 23°42'S 133°52'E |
| Al Lādhiqīyah | 60 D4 | 35°31'N 35°47'E |
| Allahabad | 63 E4 | 25°27'N 81°50'E |
| Almaty | 58 D2 | 43°19'N 76°55'E |
| Aln | 32 C7 | 55°30'N 2°0'W |
| Altai Mountains | 64 C4 | 48°0'N 88°36'E |
| Altun Shan | 64 C3 | 37°20'N 87°13'E |
| Amazon | 90 B6 | 0°10'S 49°0'W |
| Amazon Basin | 90 C6 | 4°48'S 62°44'W |
| Amazon, Mouths of the | 90 D6 | 1°0'N 48°0'W |
| Ambleside | 32 C5 | 54°26'N 2°58'W |
| Ambon | 69 F1 | 3°41'S 128°10'E |
| Amindivi Islands | 62 D1 | 11°0'N 73°0'E |
| Amman | 60 D3 | 31°57'N 35°56'E |
| Āmol | 61 F4 | 36°31'N 52°24'E |
| Amritsar | 63 E5 | 31°38'N 74°55'E |
| Amsterdam | 43 E4 | 52°22'N 4°54'E |
| Amundsen Gulf | 80 C3 | 70°42'N 124°1'W |
| Amur | 65 F5 | 53°10'N 124°52'E |
| Anadyr' | 59 G5 | 64°41'N 177°22'E |
| Anadyr, Gulf of | 59 G5 | 64°0'N 178°0'W |
| Anatolia | 60 D5 | 39°43'N 44°39'E |
| Anchorage | 82 A3 | 61°13'N 149°52'W |
| Andaman Islands | 63 G2 | 12°12'N 92°0'E |
| Andaman Sea | 68 C3 | 11°0'N 108°0'E |
| Andes | 91 B4 | 2°0'N 78°0'W |
| Andorra | 42 D2 | 42°34'N 1°34'E |
| Angel Falls | 90 C6 | 5°52'N 62°19'W |
| Anglesey | 33 A4 | 53°32'N 4°40'W |
| Angola | 52 D3 | 11°8'S 19°25'E |
| Anguilla | 85 G3 | 18°26'N 63°0'W |
| Ankara | 60 D5 | 39°55'N 32°50'E |
| An Nafud | 61 E3 | 28°14'N 40°42'E |
| An Najaf | 61 E3 | 31°59'N 44°19'E |
| Annapurna | 63 F4 | 28°30'N 83°50'E |
| Anshan | 65 F4 | 41°6'N 122°58'E |
| Antakya | 60 D4 | 36°12'N 36°10'E |
| Antalya | 60 C4 | 36°53'N 30°42'E |
| Antananarivo | 53 G2 | 18°52'S 47°30'E |
| Antarctica | 92 B3 | 90°0'S 0°0' |

| | | |
|---|---|---|
| Antigua and Barbuda | 85 H2 | 17°21'N 61°48'W |
| Antrim | 35 D4 | 54°43'N 6°13'W |
| Antrim Mountains | 35 D5 | 55°10'N 6°10'W |
| A'nyemaqen Shan | 64 D3 | 34°11'N 100°54'E |
| Aomori | 67 F4 | 40°50'N 140°43'E |
| Aoraki (Mount Cook) | 75 G1 | 43°39'S 170°5'E |
| Aoukâr | 50 B3 | 18°6'N 9°28'W |
| Appalachian Mountains | 83 G3 | 34°53'N 84°28'W |
| Arabian Peninsula | 61 E2 | 22°22'N 44°32'E |
| Arabian Sea | 62 D2 | 15°0'N 65°0'E |
| Arafura Sea | 74 D5 | 9°0'S 135°0'E |
| Araguaia, Rio | 90 D5 | 5°21'S 48°41'W |
| Aral Sea | 58 C2 | 44°34'N 59°49'E |
| Aran Islands | 35 B3 | 53°15'N 10°1'W |
| Ararat, Mount | 61 E5 | 39°43'N 44°19'E |
| Aras | 61 E5 | 39°18'N 45°7'E |
| Archangel | 44 C6 | 64°32'N 40°40'E |
| Arctic Ocean | 93 B3 | 90°0'N 0°0' |
| Ardabil | 61 E4 | 38°15'N 48°18'E |
| Ardnamurchan, Point of | 34 B3 | 56°42'N 6°16'W |
| Ards Peninsula | 35 D4 | 54°30'N 5°20'W |
| Argentina | 91 B2 | 35°54'S 64°55'W |
| Argun | 65 F5 | 50°52'N 119°31'E |
| Århus | 41 B2 | 56°9'N 10°11'E |
| Arizona | 82 D3 | 34°8'N 112°7'W |
| Arkansas | 83 F3 | 34°56'N 92°14'W |
| Arklow | 35 D3 | 52°48'N 6°9'W |
| Armagh | 35 D4 | 54°15'N 6°33'W |
| Armenia | 61 E5 | 40°36'N 44°22'E |
| Arnhem Land | 74 D4 | 14°3'S 133°24'E |
| Arran, Isle of | 34 B2 | 55°57'N 5°24'W |
| Aruba | 85 G2 | 12°30'N 69°55'W |
| Aru, Kepulauan | 69 G1 | 6°10'S 134°20'E |
| Asadabad | 58 C1 | 34°52'N 71°9'E |
| Asahi-dake | 67 F5 | 43°42'N 142°50'E |
| Asahikawa | 67 F5 | 43°46'N 142°23'E |
| Asansol | 63 F3 | 23°40'N 86°59'E |
| Aşgabat | 58 C2 | 37°58'N 58°22'E |
| Ashford | 31 G3 | 51°9'N 0°52'E |
| Asmara | 51 G3 | 15°15'N 38°58'E |
| 'Assal, Lac | 51 G3 | 11°2'N 41°51'E |
| Astana | 58 D2 | 51°13'N 71°25'E |
| Astrakhan' | 45 D3 | 46°20'N 48°1'E |
| Asunción | 91 C4 | 25°17'S 57°36'W |

| | | |
|---|---|---|
| Aswân | 51 F3 | 24°3'N 32°5'E |
| Atacama Desert | 91 B4 | 21°39'S 69°24'W |
| Athabasca, Lake | 80 D2 | 59°7'N 110°0'W |
| Athens | 45 B2 | 37°59'N 23°44'E |
| Athlone | 35 C3 | 53°25'N 7°56'W |
| Atlantic Ocean | 8 | 0°0' 40°0'W |
| Atlas Mountains | 50 C4 | 33°11'N 2°56'W |
| Atyrau | 58 C2 | 47°7'N 51°56'E |
| Auckland | 75 G1 | 36°53'S 174°46'E |
| Augusta | 83 H5 | 44°20'S 69°44'W |
| Austin | 83 E2 | 30°16'N 97°45'W |
| Australia | 74 D3 | 25°0'S 135°0'E |
| Australian Capital Territory | 75 E2 | 35°27'S 148°52'E |
| Austria | 43 F3 | 47°28'N 12°3'E |
| Aviemore | 34 C3 | 57°6'N 4°1'W |
| Avon | 31 E4 | 52°18'N 1°34'W |
| Axel Heiberg Island | 80 D4 | 79°34'N 91°16'W |
| Aydın | 60 C4 | 37°51'N 27°51'E |
| Ayers Rock see Uluru | | |
| Ayre, Point of | 32 A5 | 54°25'N 4°23'W |
| Azerbaijan | 61 E5 | 41°7'N 47°10'E |
| Aẕ Ẕahrān | 61 F3 | 26°18'N 50°2'E |

## B

| | | |
|---|---|---|
| Badlands | 83 E4 | 43°45'N 102°31'W |
| Baffin Bay | 81 E4 | 72°38'N 71°43'W |
| Baffin Island | 81 E3 | 70°7'N 73°41'W |
| Baghdâd | 61 E4 | 33°20'N 44°26'E |
| Bahamas | 85 F3 | 23°50'N 76°55'W |
| Bahrain | 61 F3 | 26°0'N 50°33'E |
| Baikal, Lake | 59 F3 | 53°0'N 108°0'E |
| Baku | 61 F5 | 40°24'N 49°51'E |
| Balabac Strait | 69 E3 | 7°37'N 116°42'E |
| Balearic Islands | 42 D1 | 39°2'N 3°1'E |
| Bali | 69 E1 | 8°18'S 115°12'E |
| Balıkesir | 60 C5 | 39°38'N 27°52'E |
| Balkhash, Lake | 58 D2 | 46°17'N 74°22'E |
| Baltic Sea | 41 C2 | 54°37'N 12°11'E |
| Baltimore | 83 H4 | 39°17'N 76°37'W |
| Bamako | 50 B2 | 12°39'N 8°2'W |
| Bananga | 63 H1 | 6°57'N 93°54'E |
| Bandar-e 'Abbas | 61 G3 | 27°11'N 56°1'E |

**Picture Credits**

The Publisher would like to thank the following for their kind permission to reproduce their photographs: (Abbreviations key: t = top, b = bottom, l = left, r = right, c = centre)

**11:** Photolibrary.com (t); **14:** Keith Ronnholm (t); **15:** Corbis/Jose Fuste Raga (tl), Corbis/Mike Theiss/Jim Reed Photography (tr), Getty/AFP (c); **16:** Alamy/ Stockfolio (tl), Corbis/Jeffrey L. Rotman (tr), Robert Harding Picture Library/Volvox (cl), Robert Harding Picture Library/Tony Waltham (b); **17:** Robert Harding Picture Library (cb, b), Corbis/Jeffrey L. Rotman (tl), Photolibrary.com (cr); **19:** www.gesource. co.uk/N.A.S.A. Visible Earth; **22:** Getty/Yukio Otsuki (cl), Panos/Qilai Shen (tr), Corbis/David Arky (c); **27:** Corbis/Reuters (tr); **28:** Empics (br); **30:** Alamy/ Photofusion Picture (tl); **31:** Corbis/Jason Hawkes (tl), Robert Harding Picture Library/Sebastian Keep (bl); **32:** Robert Harding Picture Library/Roy Rainford (t), Getty/ David Noton (c); **33:** Alamy/James Hughes; **35:** Corbis/ Peter Hulme, Ecoscene; **37:** Corbis/Philippe Giraud; **38:** www.epsaweb.org (European Primary Schools Association) (tl), Empics (bl), Science Photo Library/M-sat Ltd. (br); **39:** Science Photo Library/N.A.S.A. (tl), Science Photo Library/M-sat Ltd (tr), Science Photo Library/Space Imaging Europe (b); **40:** Corbis/Hans Strand; **41:** Corbis/Chris Lisle; **42:** Getty/Peter Adams; **43:** Robert Harding Picture Library/Adam Woolfitt (t), Robert Harding Picture Library/Michael Newton (b); **44:** Corbis/Igor Kostin (c), Corbis/ML Sinibaldi (bl); **46:** Still Pictures/Jorgen Schytte (c); **47:** Dr. Stephen Scoffham; **48:** Science Photo Library/Planetary Visions (tl), Rex Features/Sipa (bl), Science Photo Library/W.T. Sullivan 111 (br); **49:** Science Photo Library/Distribution Spot Image (tl), www.gesource.co.uk (tr), N.A.S.A. Visible Earth (bl), Science Photo Library/N.A.S.A. (br); **50:** Alamy/David Lyons; **51:** Robert Harding Picture Library/Digital Vision; **52:** Robert Harding Picture Library/DH Webster (c), Dr. Stephen Scoffham (b); **53:** Robert Harding Picture Library/Travel Library; **54:** Dr. Stephen Scoffham; **55:** Dr. Stephen Scoffham; **56:** Science Photo Library/M-sat Ltd (tl), Science Photo Library/Peter Menzel (bl), Science Photo Library/M-sat Ltd. (br); **57:** www.gesource.co.uk (tl, tr), Science Photo Library/Digital Globe, Eurimage (bl, br); **58:** Robert Harding Picture Library/Chris Rennie; **59:** Corbis/Staffan Widstrand (tl), Corbis/Viviane Moos (c), Corbis/Grigory Dukor/Reuters (b); **62:** Dr. Stephen Scoffham; **63:** Dr. Stephen Scoffham; **64:** Alamy/Danita Delimont (tr), Alamy/Stockfolio (bl); **65:** Getty/Walter Bibikow; **66:** Robert Harding Picture Library/Tony Waltham; **67:** Getty/Jeremy Woodhouse; **68:** Robert Harding Picture Library/Fraser Hall; **69:** Robert Harding Picture Library/Digital Vision (l), Corbis/Chris Lisle (r); **70:** Lonely Planet Images/Michael Aw; **71:** Alamy/Johan Elzenga; **72:** Science Photo Library/M-sat Ltd. (tl), Science Photo Library/W.T Sullivan 111 (br), Science Photo Library/US Department of Energy (bl); **73:** Science Photo Library/Space Imaging (tl), Science Photo Library/Space Imaging (bl), Science Photo Library/2002 Orbital Imaging Corporation (br); **74:** Science Photo Library/Space Imaging (c), Corbis/Matthieu Paley (b); **76:** Corbis/Alan Schein; **77:** Corbis/Tibor Bognár; **78:** Science Photo Library/Planetary Visions Ltd (tr), www.darksky.org (bl), Corbis/Bisson Bernard (br); **79:** USGS/N.A.S.A. Earthshots (tl), Science Photo Library/CNES, 1996 Distribution Spot Image (tr), USGS/N.A.S.A. Earthshots (bl), N.A.S.A. (br); **80:** Robert Harding Picture Library/Travel Library; **81:** Corbis/Hubert Stadler; **82:** Corbis/David Muench; **83:** Corbis/Eric Nguyen/Jim Reed Photography; **84:** Corbis/Peter M. Wilson (bl), Robert Harding Picture Library/Travel Library (tr); **85:** Robert Harding/Travel Library; **86:** Corbis/Mariana Bazo; **87:** Getty/Altrendo Nature; **88:** Science Photo Library/Planetary Visions (tl), Corbis/Jeremy Horner (bl), Science Photo Library/M-sat Ltd. (br); **89:** Science Photo Library/CNES, 1995 Distribution Spot Image (tl), Science Photo Library/CNES, 2002 Distribution Spot Image (b); **90:** Science Photo Library/BSIP, M.I.G./BAEZA; **91:** Robert Harding Picture Library/Chris Rennie; **95:** Panos/Clive Shirley (tl), Panos/Giacomo Pirozzi (cl), Corbis/Rolf Bruderer (cb), Panos/Barbara Klass (tr), Corbis/Frans Lanting (cr), Corbis/Kevin Coombs/Reuters (br); **97:** Dr. Stephen Scoffham; **103:** Science Photo Library/Alex Bartel; **104:** Panos/Giacomo Pirozzi.

**Jacket images**
Front: Robert Harding Picture Library/Volvox (tl), Alamy/Danita Delimont (tr), Alamy/Stockfolio (bl), Alamy/David Lyons (br); Background image: Corbis/ N.A.S.A./Roger Ressmeyer. Back: Background image: Corbis/N.A.S.A./Roger Ressmeyer.

All other images © Dorling Kindersley
For further information see www.dkimages.com

**DK EDUCATION AND DK CARTOGRAPHY**

**Designer:** Clive Savage
**Senior Cartographic Editor:** Simon Mumford
**Cartographer:** Ed Merritt
**Project Manager:** Nigel Duffield
**DTP Designer:** David MacDonald

Pearson Education
Edinburgh Gate
Harlow
Essex
CM20 2JE

England and Associated Companies throughout the World

This edition © Pearson Education Limited 2006

The right of Dr. Stephen Scoffham to be identified as the author of this Work has been asserted by him in accordance with the Copyright, Designs and Patents Act of 1988.